"By turning his attention to young people, Nidhal Guessoum helps bring science to the most important group that needs to be exposed to science in Muslim societies. In doing so, he does not shy away from tackling what have long been sensitive issues, but he does it in a way that is simple, accurate, rigorous and accessible to younger people.

The diversity of topics explored makes every chapter exciting and fresh, and I hope that the book finds its way to every school and library, as I think everyone – and not just young Muslims – should read it. I hope parents keep a copy on their bookshelves, and when their children start picking it up, it may very well ignite their love for science."

MOHAMMED YAHIA
Chief Editor of Nature Middle East

"If writing is a great invention, then writing about science is a craft, and answering awkward scientific questions by children is both a craft and a gift mastered by few. In many Islamic societies, children do not ask as many awkward scientific questions as they should. When they do, their questions are often shirked and eschewed for fear that elaborate answers may bait their young minds into doubt and uncertainty. We forget that these are the preconditions for creativity and a blossoming scientific enterprise.

Nidhal Guessoum's carefully crafted book is a fresh attempt to unshackle parents and teachers from answering questions about science. It discusses a number of issues critical for budding scientists in the Islamic societies and indeed for young Muslims in general. *The Young Muslim's Guide to Modern Science* is a timely addition by an enthusiastic science communicator to the not-so extensive library of books on science and Islam. It is essential reading for young and old alike."

DR. MONEEF R. ZOU'BI
Director General, Islamic World Academy of Sciences

"Nidhal Guessoum substantiates an excellent program for science literacy to be adopted by Muslim officials and educators. Indeed, unless Muslims solve this problem of science illiteracy effectively, they cannot meaningfully deal with the various problems facing the Muslim world today, much less have a voice in global world affairs. In brief, we need books of this kind at all levels, for all age groups and in all forms of education."

PROF. ALPARSLAN AÇIKGENÇ
Professor of History of Philosophy;
Member of the Turkish Academy of Sciences

"Young readers and their parents will find Nidhal Guessoum to be the science teacher that few of us had the privilege to experience. He is patient, knowledgeable, engaging but never patronising. Like the best science writing, *The Young Muslim's Guide to Modern Science* will help to settle old debates and ignite a few new ones."

EHSAN MASOOD
Author of *Science & Islam: A History*

"This book is the first of its kind. It is accessible and easy to read; it is as if you are having a conversation with the author; it is unique in its positive approach to science and Islam. The book addresses challenges we face today in schools and everyday life. It is comprehensive without being too detailed. It gives a road map, a guide for how to handle controversial issues in science and Islam. I loved it.

I will use it as a must-read for my students. I recommend it to Muslims and non-Muslims from every age, culture, and background, to read and give as a gift."

DR. RANA DAJANI
Hashemite University, Jordan, and founder of 'We Love Reading'

"A timely and eminently readable book by the noted science scholar Nidhal Guessoum, demolishing the pseudo-science promoted by uninformed religious actors generally, but especially in parts of the Muslim world. This book corrects the absence of accessible and informed writing on the intersection of science and religion in a Muslim idiom. Well-researched, candid and laced with moral courage, it is voices like Guessoum who can counter the deficit of dignity experienced by politically and culturally traumatized young Muslims who tend to be susceptible to undignified interpretations religion and science. It is a call to arms in order to restore the link between knowledge and human dignity. It is essential reading for people across all age groups and demographics."

PROF. EBRAHIM MOOSA
Professor of Islamic Studies at the University of Notre Dame (USA),
author of *What is a Madrasa?* and *Ghazali and the Poetics of Imagination*

"In addition to keeping scholarly standards when dealing with contemporary scientific issues, Nidhal Guessoum shows high awareness of the problem of mixing modern scientific facts and theories with the prevailing religious concepts and perceptions in our contemporary Islamic societies. This rare combination makes this book a scientific guide that can contribute to the formation of the scientific mind and motivate young minds to participate and innovate, away from the ideological use and abuse of scientific knowledge."

DR. AMER AL-HAFI
Associate Professor of Religious Studies at Al-Bayt University
and Academic Advisor to the Royal Institute for Inter-Faith Studies,
Amman, Jordan

"This is a timely and urgently needed contribution from the renowned scientist Dr. Guessoum, who is best known for expressing his convictions and well-formulated positions in an unequivocal way. I strongly recommend the book for all those interested in knowing more about the relevance of science to contemporary Muslim societies, whether they may agree or disagree with the author."

PROF. MOHAMMED GHALY
Professor of Islam and Biomedical Ethics, Research Center for Islamic Legislation & Ethics, College of Islamic Studies, Hamad Bin Khalifa University, Qatar

"Accurate and written with style, this book by Prof. Nidhal Guessoum is an engaging little treasure piece. Written for young Muslim minds, and in particular for students and teachers in view of its pedagogical treatment, this short work covers a whole spectrum of topics related to science, its history, methodology, and achievements. But its special value might reside in addressing the "touchy issues" related to science for the Muslim culture, such as the theory of Evolution, the climate change "controversy", the I'jaz (Qur'an's scientific "miraculousness") literature, the biotechnological revolution, etc. Some of those issues are delicate or even polemical, but the author takes the bull by the horns and handles them in a dispassionate, non-apologetic, yet respectful manner.

But make no mistake, purportedly written for young Muslims, adults (of any persuasion, in fact) would greatly benefit from this presentation. All in all, this timely book on science, only Prof. Guessoum could have written, and I would without hesitation recommend putting in the hands of one and all."

PROF. JAMAL MIMOUNI
University of Constantine, Algeria,
Vice-President of the Arab Union for Astronomy and Space Sciences

THE
YOUNG
MUSLIM'S
GUIDE TO
MODERN
SCIENCE

Published by Beacon Books and Media Ltd
Innospace
The Shed
Chester Street
Manchester
M1 5GD
UK

www.beaconbooks.net

ISBN 978-1-912356-01-0

A C.I.P. record for this book is available from the British Library

Cover design by Younes Boudiaf http://www.younesboudiaf.com/ and Bipin Mistry.

THE
YOUNG
MUSLIM'S
GUIDE TO
MODERN
SCIENCE

Nidhal Guessoum

Acknowledgements

First and foremost, I wish to thank my wife, Tass, for giving me all the time and quiet space I have needed for this book and other projects.

Several people have helped improve the book by carefully reading it, pointing out simple or subtle errors, proposing edits on a number of sentences and paragraphs, and suggesting clarifications on several points: my son Omar, my friend Aedan Lake, and Sheima Rafiq. Special thanks also go to Yasmeen Hamoudha and Younes Boudiaf for the superb illustrations and graphic work.

I also thank Ehsan Masood and Jamil Chishti who have been instrumental in getting this book published.

I am also grateful to and honoured by the endorsements that Moneef Zou'bi, Ebrahim Moosa, Alparslan Açıkgenç, Rana Dajani, Ehsan Masood, Jamal Mimouni, Mohammed Yahia, Mohammed Ghaly, and Amer Al-Hafi, have made for this book; may it live up to the expectations that we all have for it.

And lastly, I thank the countless people who everyday encourage me and help me spread correct knowledge and fine education and culture.

Table of Contents

....

CHAPTER 1

Introduction:
Science in Today's Muslim Culture

"And say, O my Lord! Advance me in knowledge..."

– Qur'an (20:114)

"An hour's contemplation (or study) of nature is better than a year's adoration (of God)."

– Prophet Muhammad (PBUH)

"If you want this world, seek knowledge; if you want the hereafter, seek knowledge, and if you want both, seek knowledge."

– Arabic saying attributed to several classical scholars

"We need science education to produce scientists, but we need it equally to create literacy in the public. Man has a fundamental urge to comprehend the world about him, and science gives today the only world picture which we can consider as valid... An educated layman can, of course, not contribute to science, but can enjoy and participate in many scientific discoveries which are constantly made... Literacy in science will enrich a person's life."

– Hans Albrecht Bethe (Nobel Prize winner in Physics, 1967)

Science and Islam Mixed up

IN FEBRUARY 2015, A 3-MINUTE video segment by a Saudi cleric went viral and was discussed in all media, from the New York Times to Facebook and Twitter. The topic and the statements were rather shocking: 'Earth does not move,' Sheikh Bandar al-Khaibari told an assembly of listeners, many of them university students, in the

UAE; it does not rotate around itself and does not revolve around the Sun. He presented both religious and scientific 'proofs' for his claims: First, he said, Allah created the heavenly house (al bayt al-ma`mur) directly above the Kaaba, and if the earth rotated, the heavenly house would be forced to rotate; secondly, if the earth rotated, a plane would never reach China; in fact, a plane should just take off vertically and wait for China to come under it! He further dismissed 'scientific claims' off hand: "they say they went to the moon, but it's all Hollywood stuff…"

Needless to say, the media went gaga, with articles and posts titled "Forget Copernicus"; "Move over, Galileo"; "Saudi cleric 'proves' the Earth does not rotate"; "Saudi cleric declares fascinating new theory"; and on and on. Just on YouTube, the video was watched some 200,000 times in its first week, and a Google search for 'Al-Khaibari + Earth' produced some 100,000 hits within a week.

Some commentators tried to downplay the sheikh's statements and viewpoint by pointing to recent surveys showing that even in the US, 25% of the population believes that the sun goes around the earth, not the other way around. But that ignorance is not based on 'religious knowledge' and is not being promoted and supported by a cleric and presented to an educated audience.

In fact, anyone familiar with contemporary Islamic writings knows that while Al-Khaibari's claim is rare among Muslim scholars nowadays, there are a number of prominent Saudi clerics (the famous Sheikh Bin Baz, Sheikh Al-Tuwaijri, Sheikh Al-Fawzan, and others) who in recent times have insisted that Earth is stationary and that anyone who claims that it rotates around itself or revolves around the sun or wants this to be taught is a heretic. Fatwas (scholarly Islamic opinions) have been issued on this, but everyone has more or less ignored them, and the rotation and revolution of Earth as a planet has been taught to all students everywhere, including in Saudi Arabia… Still, the Arab Twittersphere (largely dominated by Saudi youngsters) is full of 'sceptics' or 'rejectionists' of the 'western theory' that Earth rotates and revolves around the sun or that humans have set foot on the moon. This highlights the necessity of engaging in such an educational effort as this work.

Some serious discussions did take place in the wake of that story: Is this just an odd case or is this viewpoint widespread? Do Muslims widely mix up basic science with religious beliefs? Is Islam suppressing scientific literacy? Is this kind of ignorance particular to the Arab-Muslim culture or is it found elsewhere? Is it best to ignore this kind of talk or should experts respond to such 'proofs'? Why is this Muslim scholar so devoid of basic worldly knowledge? What should be done to prevent students from being mis-educated in this manner? Etc.

These are all vital questions to address, and I will go over them, briefly in this introduction, and in more depth in other chapters of this book. Indeed, this book altogether is meant to address the lack of basic, essential scientific literacy among the general public and how to construct a more solid bridge between Islam and modern science.

But before I do that, let me offer a few more examples of the kind of erroneous mixing of scientific information (often misunderstood) with Islamic beliefs.

Is the Sun about to Rise from the West?

This is a question I have received many times (through social media in particular), and it shows a similar lack of scientific (astronomical) literacy, although not as extreme as the previous example.

The question is usually formulated like this: NASA has 'announced' that the earth's magnetic field will soon flip, therefore north will become south, and east will become west; hence, the sun will be rising from the west! Of course, the person asking the question then quickly reminds me that the sun rising from the west is, according to Islamic tradition, one of the 'great signs' of the Day of Judgment; indeed, this is why this 'NASA news' resonates among the Muslim public and spreads faster than any typical rumour...

In response to the question, I first briefly explain that Earth's magnetic field flips every half million years, on average, so this is not something extraordinary, an end-of-times type of event. The flips are due to irregularities and turbulences in the electric currents inside Earth. Indeed, we have geological and fossil records showing the planet's magnetic field in different directions at various geological epochs. Such a reversal has occurred hundreds, perhaps thousands of times in our planet's geological history (of 4.5 billion years). The last time this occurred was 786,000 years ago; thus, Earth is due (perhaps overdue) for a magnetic flip.

I then explain that geologists have recently been noticing a weakening of the earth's magnetic field, and so they forecast a flip sometime in the next 1,000 or perhaps 10,000 years. Things took a sharp turn in June 2014, however, when new measurements from European Space Agency satellites were presented at a scientific conference in Denmark showing that the weakening of the magnetic field had accelerated: its strength is presently decreasing at a rate of 5% per decade instead of per century, as had previously been determined. Thus, a reversal could occur in the next 100 years instead of thousands of years. The media then reported that "the earth's magnetic field may flip during our lifetime," and someone (incorrectly) inferred that... the sun may soon rise from the west!

I should note, however, that researchers are not claiming that the magnetic field *will* soon flip, only that it *may*. Indeed, geological records show that sometimes the field weakens but does not flip. And when it does, the reversal usually takes about a century to complete!

But what if it does? What impact will it have on us and on life on Earth? Doesn't the magnetic field protect us from harmful solar particles?

A reversal does not necessarily mean that the magnetic field totally vanishes while flipping over; the field becomes chaotic, with multiple poles appearing over the planet. Moreover, the paleontological record does *not* show any past extinctions corresponding to magnetic reversal times. So while we may expect some sensitive animals to be affected by a weak magnetic field (for example, many birds will lose their 'internal compass' ability), and some humans may be more sensitive than others to magnetic variations, no large-scale disasters are likely to occur.

But going back to the original story, if and when the earth's magnetic field does flip, would the sun then be rising from the west?

That would only be true if one defines east and west using magnetic directions. For astronomers and almost everyone else, directions are set by the locations of stars and constellations around us. And since the rotation of the earth will not change in any such reversal, the sun will still arise from the geographic—though not the magnetic—east!

Indeed, we must remember that the sun's rising and setting is only an apparent effect that is due to Earth's rotation around itself. Hence, if and when the earth's magnetic field does reverse its poles, Earth's rotation will not be affected, and the sun will still rise and set in the same way as ever.

Is the Sun Rising from the West on Mars or Venus?

Another wrong connection between scientific misunderstandings and religious beliefs can be witnessed every year or so, when the media announces that "astronomers report that Mars is now moving backward". My Twitter feed then quickly fills up with questions about "the sun rising on Mars from the west" and whether that implies that the Apocalypse is near... for Earth.

This too is simply a manifestation of scientific/astronomical illiteracy. People (including the media, particularly in the Arab world where science reporters can be counted on one's fingers) confuse 'retrograde motion' with 'retrograde rotation'. The former is what Mars does very regularly: it appears to be moving backward among the stars for a few weeks, before moving forward again. Not only has it been doing this ever since the solar system formed, with all its planets, some 4.6 billion years ago, this effect can simply be explained by Earth revolving faster than Mars around the Sun (Earth takes 1 year, Mars takes 1.8 years) because Earth is closer to the sun than Mars. At a certain point, Earth 'overtakes' Mars, which then (relative to Earth) seems to be moving backward. The bottom line is: Mars doesn't do anything different than Earth, and the sun rises on the red planet from the east as it has always done.

On the other hand, Venus rotates backward (or upside down) around itself (this is 'retrograde rotation') and thus the sun rises on it from the west, and it has done so for billions of years. Nothing unusual there either, and no Apocalypse to be expected.

Other Examples of Scientific Illiteracy

A famous documentary once asked Harvard students, on the day of their graduation, why it is hotter in the summer than in the winter (in the northern hemisphere). Fewer than ten percent of them answered correctly. Indeed, the answer is not that the Earth comes closer to the Sun in the summer (in fact, the Earth is closer to the Sun in the winter of the northern hemisphere); the correct explanation is that the Earth's axis of rotation is inclined, not vertical.

Similarly, at George Mason University, half of the seniors who were surveyed could not state the difference between an atom and a molecule. Such ignorance is much more widespread in the general public, as half of the surveyed American public does not know how long it takes the earth to orbit around the sun, and one in five thinks the *sun* goes *around* the *earth*. In 2008,[1] about 28% of American adults were judged to be 'scientifically literate',[2] up from only 10% in 1988. The 2008 study covered 34 countries, most of them from Europe but also including the USA, Japan, and Turkey, the lat-

---

[1] http://ns.umich.edu/new/releases/8265; https://www.aacu.org/publications-research/periodicals/what-colleges-and-universities-need-do-advance-civic-scientific.

[2] To be classified as 'scientifically literate,' the survey required people to be able to understand 20 of 31 scientific concepts (the list can be found in the link given in the previous note) and terms similar to those that would be found in articles that appear in good newspapers or in good science TV shows.

ter having the lowest score, with only 2% of the adult population deemed 'scientifically literate' (see Figure 1).

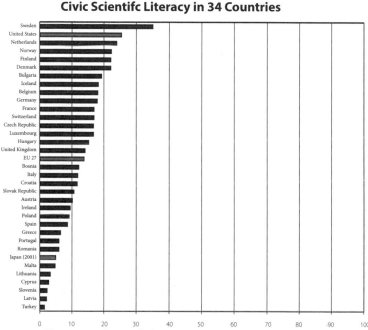

Civic Scientifc Literacy in 34 Countries

Figure 1 – *Scientific literacy in various countries (2005-2007).*

Here below are a few important examples of science literacy (or lack thereof):

- On the accuracy of the statement "It is the father's gene that de-cides whether the baby is a boy or a girl" (which is true), correct responses varied from 22% (in Russia) to 65% (in the USA), with Malaysia scoring 46%.[3] Clearly, this question has important social consequences, particularly in societies where a woman who doesn't give birth to a boy after several deliveries is sub-jected to various kinds of ill-treatment.

- On the veracity of the statement: "Antibiotics kill viruses as well as bacteria" (which is untrue), correct responses varied from

---

[3]   Science and Engineering Indicators 2006: https://www.uni-klu.ac.at/wiho/downloads/nsf_volume1.pdf

18% (in China) to 51% (in the USA), with Malaysia scoring 21%, Russia 18%, and Japan 23%.[4] This has important consequences in places where antibiotics are over-prescribed, often due to the insistence of patients, leading to 'super-strong', antibiotic-resistant bacteria (a growing problem in many hospitals). Indeed, contrary to popular beliefs, antibiotics are harmless to viruses, and prescribing them is not only a waste of resources but may cause other existing bacteria to develop resistance to these antibiotics.

- Discussions of genetically modified foods and organisms and of stem-cell research and its applications have become commonplace. Obviously, a basic familiarity and understanding of these terms and the issues they raise is essential for a proper discussion, particularly on the part of educated people, religious leaders, and policymakers. In fact, soon we will have to address much more challenging topics such as 'synthetic life' (sometimes referred to as 'artificial life'), animal 'de-extinction' projects (bringing back dinosaurs and other animals, and perhaps in the future dead humans), technologically modified or 'augmented' or 'enhanced' humans (sometimes referred to as 'transhumanism'), and even 'immortality'. (See the discussion of this issue with regard to Islam in Chapter 6.)

What is Science Literacy and Why is it Important?

Science literacy is the general understanding of scientific ideas (facts, terms, theories), which allows a reasonably educated person to digest scientific information that is received from various media. It also allows one to follow discussions on science-related topics (e.g. stem cell research) and come to an informed conclusion.

This competency is supposed to be produced by the general science courses that all students receive, partly in high school and partly in college. In fact, the latest big improvements noted above for US adults in science literacy has been attributed to the fact that US universities require all non-science majors to take one to three

---

4   Ibid.

science courses.[5] Indeed, college students majoring in the humanities in Japan and Europe are not required to take science courses, thus the very low science literacy scores in Japan in particular.

According to Jon Miller,[6] the second biggest factor contributing to adult scientific literacy is informal science education resources, which include: science articles in newspapers and magazines, science web-

> *Increasingly, our leaders must deal with dangers that threaten the entire world, where an understanding of those dangers and the possible solutions depends on a good grasp of science. The ozone layer, the greenhouse effect, acid rain, questions of diet and heredity. All require scientific literacy.*
>
> *– Isaac Asimov*

sites, visits to museums, regular attendance of public libraries, and reading general science books. According to surveys presented in the Science and Engineering Indicators of 2006,[7] the internet quickly became and continues to be the largest contributing source to scientific information in the U.S. and many other countries worldwide. In fact, much of the scientific 'information' is received inadvertently, either through news stories or entertainment programmes. And while this makes scientific information readily available to everyone, the lack of ability to sift through accurate material from junk has further complicated the science literacy situation.

---

[5] See Jon D. Miller, Civic Scientific Literacy: A Necessity for the 21st Century. Public Interest Report: Journal of the Federation of American Scientists, 55:1:3-6. 2002; Jon D. Miller and Rafael Pardo. "Civic scientific literacy and attitude to science and technology: A comparative analysis of the European Union, the United States, Japan, and Canada." *Between understanding and trust: The public, science and technology* (2000): 131-156.

[6] Jon Miller was (from 1991 to 2000) Vice-President of the Chicago Academy of Sciences, and Director of the International Center for the Advancement of *Scientific Literacy; see references in previous footnote.*

[7] Science and Engineering Indicators 2006: https://wayback.archive-it. org/5902/20160210153725/http://www.nsf.gov/statistics/seind06/

Science literacy has become more and more important these days, as information spreads more quickly than ever. If the public is not equipped with the basic information that allows it to filter correct information from wild rumours, much time, effort, and energy will be wasted in correcting such stories. Moreover, panics may occur among the public (as we may recall from the 2012 Mayan 'apocalypse' craze) and people may resort to irrational solutions (e.g. buy special 'products') that will help them deal with the situation, at least psychologically. Indeed, a scientifically cultured population is less likely to fall victim to fraudulent claims and schemes, from astrology to sham cures.

Science Literacy Objectives

Having realised the importance and value of science literacy, and before we launch into a programme of reviewing the main scientific ideas that any educated person must hold in the twenty-first century and how they can nicely be harmonised with one's religious/Islamic culture, we need to set the objectives for such a programme. In other words, what exactly do we aim to achieve?

My university, which requires students from all fields (including humanities, social sciences, and languages) to complete at least two full courses in basic sciences, sets the following goals for such a science literacy programme:[8]

➢ Recognise the value of the natural and physical sciences.

➢ Explain how scientific hypotheses are conceived and tested.

➢ Explain how basic scientific concepts are related to contemporary issues.

➢ Employ quantitative reasoning as a conceptual tool for analysis and description.

➢ Analyse data to identify quantitative and qualitative relationships

---

[8] https://www.aus.edu/info/200228/general_education_program/468/program_areas_and_courses/5

I can perhaps give a more detailed set of goals for science literacy, ideas that apply more to the general public's knowledge:

✓ To have a greater understanding of the role of science in society and in everyday life.

✓ To distinguish between scientific theories, laws, hypotheses, observations, models, facts, concepts, and terminology.

✓ To be able to describe and explain natural phenomena using scientific reasoning, at least qualitatively.

✓ To be familiar with the present state of scientific knowledge and current issues in science.

✓ To recognise the progressive and cumulative nature of science, building on past advances by small steps (mostly) and occasionally making big jumps/shifts.

✓ To recognise the gaps in many areas of scientific knowledge, the limits of what is or can be known on certain topics, and the probabilistic nature of knowledge in some fields.

✓ To be able to analyse scientific information that is presented, beyond mere 'facts'.

✓ To distinguish scientific information from the ethical, judicial, and socio-political aspects of a topic and recognise situations that require a consideration of several of these aspects.

✓ To fully appreciate why research is sometimes conducted for basic scientific reasons.

Needless to say, in the next chapters we will discuss many if not all of these ideas, including what we call scientific 'facts' and 'theories', as well as concepts and methods.

But for now and practically speaking, let's say that a scientifically literate person should be able to:[9]

• Distinguish science from pseudo-science such as astrology, quackery, and schemes that aim to fleece people by taking advantage of their ignorance, their fears, and needs in their lives.

---

[9]   Partly adapted from Paul DeHart Hurd, "Scientific Literacy: New Minds for a Changing World", *Science Education*, Vol. 82, Issue 3. pp. 407–416, June 1998

- Distinguish reliable expert knowledge from uninformed ideas propagated in unreliable venues. This entails having the capacity to assess the quality of information sources such as websites, newspapers and television programmes, and adequately use multiple sources...

- Distinguish evidenced-based and data-supported propositions from old, long-held views and 'received wisdom'.

- Recognise when a cause and effect relationship should not be drawn from a set of data – and become familiar with the idea that "correlation is not causation".

- Understand how scientific research is conducted, how scientific findings are reviewed and validated, and how institutional pronouncements are to be distinguished from individual proclamations.

- Use scientific knowledge where appropriate in making choices and decisions, forming judgments, resolving problems, and taking action.

A more sophisticated understanding of scientific information and ideas would include:

- Understanding the role of the peer review process in the scientific community and how it helps ascertain scientific knowledge.

- Recognising when arguments are flawed, either because facts and opinions are being mixed or the conclusions being drawn do not follow logically from the evidence given.

- Knowing that one or two examples cannot be generalised to a statement claiming something to always be true, but that sometimes a single example can show that some claim is false or at least not always true.

- Having basic understanding of statistical methods, starting with sample effects (size and randomness), error bars, mean, median, standard deviations, biases, etc.

To acquire a basic understanding of the formulation of research studies (proper hypotheses, designs of research, etc.) and what conclusions can be drawn in various cases. But in real life, how does such scientific literacy benefit people? It allows them to understand contemporary science and public policy information and debates on vital issues, such as:[10]

- Health (biological, behavioural, social, environmental) matters: new drugs, control of epidemics, pandemics, cancer studies and treatments, sexually transmitted diseases, gene therapies, stem-cell research, etc.

- Environmental issues and policies: climate change, ecological policies, environmental protection, biodiversity, species extinction, etc.

- Important topics of food and agriculture: genetically modified foods/organisms, biotechnology, etc.

- Energy debates: renewable sources, pollution and other impacts, biofuels, etc.

- Demographics and population dynamics: population growths in different countries, migration, etc.

This has become an important subject of discussion among educators, and indeed in the last few decades, academic journals addressing issues at the interface of science, education, culture, and social trends have appeared, including: *Cultural Studies of Science Education, Science, Technology & Human Values, Science and Education, Social Studies of Science, and others.*

Scientific (II)Literacy and Muslim Culture

Muslims often insist that Islam has never had a problem with science, and that a problematic relation exists only in western culture due to the Church's old suspicion and 'oppression' of science, such as in the Galileo affair. Muslims invariably cite many Qur'anic verses to support the idea of Islam's encouragement of Science, from the very first word revealed to Prophet Muhammad, "*Iqra*" ("Read/Recite!" – 96:1) to "*Truly fear Allah those among His Servants who have knowledge*" (35:28).

---

[10] See a much longer and more detailed list in Paul DeHart Hurd, "Scientific Literacy: New Minds for a Changing World", *Science Education*, Vol. 82, Issue 3, pp. 407–416, June 1998.

However, except for Turkey's participation in the science literacy survey I reported above, there have not been any studies of the problem in the Arab-Muslim world. Still, knowledge of the cultural landscape (media, education, academia) of today's Muslim world, or at least the Arab world, indicates a complex spectrum of attitudes. The extreme variety of Islamic views and practices (ranging from Daesh to the growing trend of atheism in the region) should be quite obvious to anyone who follows the Arab-Muslim society – superficial western media notwithstanding. But probably much less known is the range of attitudes and levels of knowledge regarding science that can be found when one looks a bit closer.

In fact, over the past few years in the Arab-Muslim world, we have witnessed the return of a religion-based anti-science standpoint. This is exemplified by high clerics making various statements that simply reject well-established scientific knowledge, insisting that the Qur'an be taken literally and that science is just a western scheme aiming to impose a materialistic worldview. This fundamentalist, anti-modernist, and anti-science movement is worrisome because it tells young Muslims today that they must choose between science and Islam. Indeed, we have seen articles published recently in the Muslim world with titles such as "Science and religion don't always agree." If that is the case, then we have a lose-lose situation: either youngsters choose a close-minded version of Islam and reject the modern world (the Daesh route), or they choose science and modernity and reject religion…

I sometimes hear the view that one should just brush aside such ignorant anti-science proclamations. I do not agree with that approach. On the contrary, I believe we need to discuss all such claims and pronouncements in the open and provide strong arguments to convince students and the public that science must be taken seriously and that Islam does not clash with it. Otherwise, many youngsters will be exposed only to the anti-science/anti-modern viewpoint, and many have become convinced by it, not having heard the opposing arguments. It is unfortunate that in the 21st

century we have to explain the earth's motion to the public, but we cannot take the risk of fundamentalism growing further.

But why do some religious scholars carry such ignorance about what is in fact taught in elementary schools? I think it is due to the closed and largely obsolete curriculum that is taught in Islamic madrasas/institutes, at least in some countries (Saudi Arabia and Pakistan being prominent examples).

Reforms of the curricula are urgently needed, whereby not only must basic science (astronomy, geology, biology) be taught to future Muslim scholars, but also ideas such as hermeneutics (intelligent interpretation of the scriptures) and critical analysis, so that clerics learn how to deal with topics where they may encounter some apparent conflicts. Indeed, the literalist approach to sacred texts (in Islam and other religions) has produced dangerous views and attitudes on many aspects of society and culture.

Had the Sheikh Al-Khaibari studied some basic physics and astronomy, not to mention different interpretations of the Qur'anic verses he cited, he would not have voiced his laughable 'proof' of why Earth cannot be rotating around itself or revolving around the sun...

The Moral of the Story(ies)

So what do we learn from the stories and surveys that I have related in this introductory chapter? First and foremost, that there is a huge need for improved scientific literacy in the Arab-Muslim world. It is unacceptable to have educated people still debating whether the earth revolves around the sun or the other way around, or whether the earth rotates around itself at all. While it is true that this problem is not limited to Muslims and that science illiteracy is still a major issue around the world, there have been significant improvements elsewhere, thanks to efforts by societies for the advancement of science, by educators and policymakers, public literacy programmes through media, museums, and such. Our part of the world needs similar important initiatives.

I have succinctly explained why scientific literacy is a must in our world today: almost all innovations and changes in our lifestyles are brought about by scientific and technological developments; discoveries are happening every day and at an accelerated pace; simply understanding what is happening and what it means to us requires at least basic scientific knowledge; many policy issues that are debated in society (what to do about global warming, what policy we should adopt with regard to genetic engineering, etc.) require citizens to be scientifically informed; and last but not least, particularly within the Muslim culture, a number of these issues raise religious concerns, and one must first understand the topic correctly before trying to figure out an appropriate religious position on it.

I also briefly outlined the basic principles of scientific literacy that should be sought: what do we want the public to know and understand about science? It is not just a bunch of facts (how old is the earth, how old is the universe, what is a gene, etc.), although some minimum knowledge of such facts is important. It is also and perhaps most importantly an understanding of the difference between scientific 'facts', 'laws', 'theories', 'hypotheses', and 'models', how science functions (the 'scientific models', in theory and in practice), the limitations and intrinsic shortcomings of science, and last but not least how to assess a piece of information that one receives from one source (e.g. the media) or another (books, lectures, etc.).

In the following chapters, I firstly present to the reader a brief history of science, showing how it evolved to take its 'modern' form. I then devote a chapter to explain what this 'modern science' really is and how it works, as well as the critiques that have been levelled at it. The next chapter then summarises "all the (basic) science that you should know" and "what remains to be known". I then review "what Islam has to say about those topics" and "Islam and Science in our future world", from the Big Bang and Evolution to climate change and genetic engineering, showing where the points of friction are and how they can be resolved, insisting that what is strongly established by science must be taken on board by Muslims as by everyone else, and emphasising the rich possibilities of interpretations of Islamic texts to accord with facts of nature, which constitute another form of divine revelation. I conclude the book with a brief summary of the main scientific information that I presented and what the reader should take away, as well as a prescription for "how not to be mistaken" (i.e. how to avoid falling for erroneous claims), in addition to some reflections on what science brings to humans and why science should care about religion.

I wish you an enjoyable and beneficial reading.

························

CHAPTER 2

A Brief History of Science

*"The ink of the scholar is more sacred
than the blood of the martyr."*

– *Prophet Muhammad (PBUH)*

*"What is a scientist after all? It is a curious man looking through
a keyhole, the keyhole of nature, trying to know what's going on."*

– *Jacques Cousteau*

The Nature of Science and its Evolution

FIRSTLY, WE NEED TO DEFINE 'SCIENCE'. In the Arabic-Islamic vocabulary, the word for 'science' is `ilm, which is the same one used for 'knowledge'. Indeed, `ilm encompasses all forms of knowledge, including 'revealed knowledge', i.e. scriptures, religious knowledge, which is constructed from scriptures, prophetic statements and actions, scholarly deliberations and pronouncements, and so forth. It also includes social sciences and humanities, e.g. history.

However, today when the word 'science' is used, it most often refers to natural science, our attempts at understanding nature and the cosmos and the descriptions and explanations of how and why things work this or that way.

Such attempts at understanding how the world around us works go back to the dawn of humanity. Since the earliest times, and from what we can gather from cave paintings and drawings on rocks, dried animal skins and bones, and other records, humans have always been fascinated by natural phenomena, particularly celestial ones: moon phases, meteors, comets, etc. Humans also noticed regularities in nature: the sun rises and sets every 24 hours, roughly, the moon goes through phases over a month's period, stars and constellations appear in certain daylight and yearly cycles, etc. For thousands of years, humans have wondered about these phenomena. So one might say that natural science goes back to the earliest days of humanity.

With human intellectual progress, we came to understand that explanations of phenomena must be governed by some principles and methods: one cannot simply proclaim an explanation, no matter how 'knowledgeable' or 'authoritative' one may be; one must present evidence and justifications for that claim. Indeed, in the most recent understanding of how science must proceed, one must propose a way for testing and ascertaining one's claim, a way for others to check the veracity of the claim. This is called 'falsifiability' and was introduced by the Austrian philosopher of science Karl Popper in the 1930s.

So today, one can define natural science as a body of knowledge about the world that is methodical, rigorous, empirical (based on observations and experiments), and objective (does not depend on who does the experiment, observation, calculation, or simulation).

Science has also been transformed over the last few centuries; it underwent a 'scientific revolution' and became 'modern'. I will explain later how 'modern science' is fundamentally different from medieval, ancient or primitive forms of science. For instance, one may note that the word *scientist* is quite recent: it was first coined by William Whewell in the 19th century. Before that, people exploring nature in a 'scientific' way were called natural philosophers. It is thus important to review the evolution of science to its contemporary form and how and why it sometimes elicits objections and rejections from some people.

One related question should be addressed before I present a brief history of science: does science make continuous, incremental progress, or does it make jumps, through big discoveries that transform the heretofore assembled body of knowledge? For a long time, indeed until the mid-20th century, science was seen as making steady progress, one step at a time, one brick or layer on top of another. However, Thomas Kuhn, the 20th century historian and philosopher of science, shook things up when, in his ground-breaking work *The Structure of Scientific Revolutions*, argued that science goes through a period of 'normal science' when a dominant 'paradigm' is worked on incrementally by everyone, but then the appearance and accumulation of anomalies sometimes forces a serious overhaul of a dominant paradigm (in one particular field), at which point a 'revolution' occurs: a new paradigm replaces the old one. Hence, we can say that science generally progresses in a continuous manner but sometimes undergoes jumps. The graph below represents roughly how I like to describe science's progress toward 'truths':

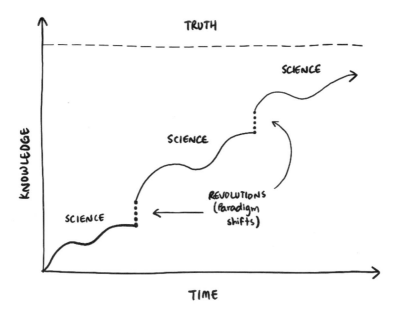

Figure 2 – *Schematic of how science progresses toward truth(s).*

Ancient Science (3rd Millennium BC – 6th c. AD)

Historians tell us that records of both natural phenomena and social activity among various peoples on Earth show some interesting common trends.

First, essential and advanced knowledge of geometry seems to have emerged rather quickly, with the Pythagoras theorem (the square of the hypotenuse of a right triangle is equal to the sum of the squares of the other two sides) being known and used by a number of cultures and civilisations, from Asia and the Middle East to Europe.

Secondly, astronomy was—for obvious reasons—the first bona fide 'science' to emerge everywhere, from China to the Americas. Indeed, the sky presented itself as an every-day and every-night spectacle of order, regularity, beauty, and awe, calling for some form of understanding, explanation, or interpretation.

Thirdly, science in general and astronomy in particular was almost always intertwined with religion. Humans always believed that natural and cosmic phenomena are signs for us from 'above', and that one must relate the 'scientific' description of any phenomena with its meaning. This intimate relation between science and religion was actually quite a fruitful one, as natural/cosmic phenomena were related to religious rituals, which then needed to be organised, which in turn spurred the growth of astronomy/astrology, which required more and more advanced mathematics.

The Egyptian (pharaonic) civilisation made substantial advances in mathematics, astronomy, and medicine. Geometry was first needed for land surveying, particularly with the Nile floods regularly washing away boundaries between properties. Geometry's importance was amplified by the huge construction projects that went on for centuries, i.e. the pyramids and the temples. Egypt was also known for its mastery of alchemy and medicine, with ointments, cures, and mummification techniques, all of which spurred increasing investigation and advancement of some aspects of the natural sciences.

Another civilisation which contributed greatly to the development of science was the Sumerian/Babylonian civilisation in Mesopotamia (Iraq). Beginning around 3500 BC, the Sumerians made important records of astronomical observations in thousands of clay tablets. Knowledge and application of the 'Pythagoras' theorem can be found in the records around 1800 BC. The Babylonians were also competent in astronomy, as they constructed solar and lunar calendars as well as cyclical tables to predict the appearances of the moon, the planets and eclipses.

In Greece, science emerged intertwined with philosophy, starting around the 6th or 7th century BC. Thales (640–546 BC) is often referred to as the 'father of science'. He tried to provide a 'unified' 'scientific' explanation for all observed natural phenomena (he believed that everything could be related to water in its three states, liquid, solid, and gaseous—for example, that earthquakes are caused by the agitation of the water upon which the land floats). He also believed that phenomena represent divine orders that direct things to their appointed states or ends.

Subsequently, Greek philosophers/scientists based their views and 'theories' of nature on two important principles: a) the universe is highly ordered (the word cosmos/*kósmos* means 'order'); b) the world can be understood by rational methods—hence the huge development of philosophy. Another important idea appeared in Greek philosophy: 'teleology'—that objects move toward an end that their (divinely ordained) properties dispose them to. We will later see that modern science rejected teleology and kept only the principles of order and rational methods of discovery.

One important concept that emerged among Greek philosophers and naturalists is the atom (from 'a-tomos', meaning in-divisible), representing the smallest piece of matter for any element. As early as the 5th century BC, Leucippus introduced the idea. It was later picked up and expanded by his disciple Democritus (ca. 460 – ca. 370 BC).

The Greeks' arguments that the earth is spherical
1. Ships moving toward the horizon tended to disappear rather suddenly, not gradually, implying a curving of the earth itself.
2. Early travellers noticed that when they went south (in Egypt), the positions of stars and constellations changed substantially, and in fact new ones appeared that could not be seen up North. An explanation to that, supported by simple geometry, was that Earth must be spherical.
3. Aristotle noted that the shadow of the Earth seen on the Moon during lunar eclipses clearly indicates its spherical shape.
4. Aristotle argued that physically, since solid, heavy matter tends to move toward the centre of the Earth (his version of gravity), the planet must necessarily have pulled itself into a spherical shape.
5. The sphere is the most perfect shape, hence the Earth must be spherical…

The Greeks also developed geometry and astronomy, presenting strong arguments that the earth is spherical (as early as the 6th century) and producing the famous geocentric model, which remained dominant for almost two millennia, including throughout the Islamic civilisation. Still, one must note that Aristarchus of Samos was the first to propose a heliocentric model of the solar system, placing the sun at the centre, but it was brushed aside by almost all astronomers until the 16th century. Other achievements included the geographer Eratosthenes's accurate determination of the circumference of the earth and Hipparchus (c. 190 – c. 120 BC) producing the first star catalogue. Plato and Aristotle, in addition to their huge contributions in other areas of philosophy, advanced the methodology of scientific inquiry by discussing the merits and validity of deductive vs. inductive reasoning.

Deductive reasoning is a logical step-by-step thought progression from general principles or hypotheses to specific conclusions that flow from the initial assumptions. This is generally what is done in Philosophy and in Mathematics. If the starting point is correct, then the conclusions will be true if the deductions were carried out according to the (correct) rules of logic.

Inductive reasoning, on the other hand, starts with specific observations and constructs general rules or laws from the patterns that are noticed. This is how science generally works, or at least starts: observations and patterns lead one to propose a hypothesis or law, from which implications are drawn and are then tested to check whether the proposed hypothesis or law is correct.

Aristotle also made a number of important scientific contributions, most notably in astronomy/cosmology and biology, presenting 'theories' of the heavens as well as of biological causation and the diversity of life. He made numerous observations of plants and animals, classifying hundreds of animal species and dissecting dozens of them. He was thus a prime example of a 'philosopher-scientist' who investigated huge arrays of topics and made substantial contributions to many of them.

In medicine, Hippocrates (c. 460 BC–c. 370 BC), famous for the Hippocratic Oath, which is still upheld and used today by physicians and other medical personnel, was able to describe many diseases and medical conditions. The other famous Greek physician, Galen (129 – c. 200 AD) developed a theory of the body (how organs work) and performed a number of advanced surgical operations, including on the eye and the brain.

In Alexandria (Hellenistic Egypt), the mathematician Euclid (ca. 325 BC – ca. 265 BC), often referred to as 'the father of geometry', gave mathematics a firm methodology based on axioms and theorems. Axioms are starting assumptions that are believed to be evidently true but cannot be proven; theorems are statements that can be proven, starting from the axioms and using the rules and methods of logic. His *Elements* is considered one of the greatest books ever written and is still widely used today.

Also in Egypt, Archimedes made important contributions to mathematics but is more famously known as a physicist, with his seminal work on fluids (buoyancy)[11] and statics (the basic principles of levers).

The Indian civilisation is much less widely known for its huge contributions to mathematics and science despite having spanned several millennia, from the 4th millennium BC in the Indus Valley, where relics of old constructions show some preliminary knowledge of mathematics and statics, to the 15th century AD when Nilakantha Somayaji (1444–1544), a great mathematician and astronomer at the Kerala school, produced the most sophisticated model of the heavens (planetary orbits) before Kepler's elliptical revolution.

Before that, in the 6th and 7th centuries CE, Indian scientists introduced important mathematical concepts that Arab-Muslim scientists adopted to great benefit. Aryabhata (476–550), in his *Aryabhatiya* introduced several fundamental trigonometric functions (including sine, cosine and inverse sine), trigonometric tables, and mathematical techniques and procedures. In the 7th century, Brahmagupta explained how zero was to be used as both a decimal digit and a placeholder. That numeral system (0 to 9) was adopted by Arab-Muslim scientists, starting with Al-Khwarizmi (ca. 780–ca. 850), as 'Arabic numerals' and has since been almost universally used, known as the Hindu-Arabic numeral system.

Medieval Science (6thc. AD–Mid-16thc. AD)

The Chinese civilisation also spanned several millennia, reaching up to the 'middle ages' when contact was made first with the Arab-Muslim civilisation and later with the western civilisation. Chinese scientists made wide-ranging and extraordinary discov-

---

[11] Archimedes is known to many pupils today through his 'Eureka' moment/story, when he suddenly realised in his bath why some objects float.

eries and contributions in both science and technology, including the compass, paper, the rocket and more.

While 0 was not used as a separate digit and quantity, 10 was considered a separate quantity, and by the first century BC negative numbers and decimal fractions were introduced. Later times saw Chinese mathematicians develop techniques for calculating square, cubic, and higher roots of numbers and solving linear, quadratic, and cubic equations. In algebra and geometry too, seminal developments occurred, too.

In Astronomy, Chinese observations represent the longest continuous series ever recorded of various phenomena, including eclipses, sunspots, comets, and supernovas, the most famous being the one that occurred in 1054, which produced what today can be seen as the Crab Nebula. Chinese astronomers were also competent in calculations of planetary positions and eclipse dates.

Shortly after its appearance on the world stage, Islam produced a golden age of knowledge and science that lasted a thousand years. Historians and commentators point to various factors for that explosion of activity: from the Qur'an itself, which exhorts Muslims to contemplate God's signs in the heavens and explore the earth in search of knowledge, to the hadiths, which placed scholars at the highest levels of humanity, to the religious practices (prayers, fasting, rules of financial transactions, etc.) which Islam required of its practitioners. Indeed, prayer times, the direction to Mecca, the construction of an Islamic calendar for both holy occasions (Ramadan, Eids, Hajj) and civil purposes (payment of salaries, debts, etc.), the computation of *zakat*, the division of lands and monies among heirs, etc., soon required some sophisticated astronomy, trigonometry, and algebra.

When Al-Khwarizmi composed his historic book on Algebra, *Kitab al-Jabr wal Muqabalah* (around 830 AD), he introduced it in a way that relates strongly to the religious needs of the Muslim community, "That fondness for science, by which God had distinguished Imam al-Mamun... has encouraged me to compose a short work,

... confining it to what is easiest and most useful in arithmetic, such as men constantly require in cases of inheritance, legacies, partition, law-suits, and trade, and in their dealings with one another...".[12] One example he gives is that of a woman who dies and leaves behind an estate to be inherited by her husband, her son, and her three daughters, according to the (complex) Islamic rules of inheritance. Al-Khwarizmi then shows that this problem can be turned into an algebraic equation, and simple operations allow one to find the answer for any size of the estate. He goes on to show that more complex problems, including determinations of *zakat*, can be dealt with in a similar fashion.

Historians and commentators also point to the scientific cultures that Muslims found when they moved to places like Mesopotamia and the Nile Valley, where they found sophisticated irrigation systems, complex knowledge relating to one's life[13] and advanced technical skills in areas such as textiles, leather, glass and metalworking. Once they interacted with scholars from India, Byzantium, and elsewhere, they learned systematic methods of inquiry and learning, which then became science.

Muslim scientists considered experiments the basis of science, much more so than the Greeks, who had excelled more on theoretical underpinnings and developments of the sciences. Thus, Ibn al-Haytham (ca. 965–ca.1040 AD), one of the greatest of the thousands of scientists who make up the Golden Age of the Islamic civilisation, is recognised more and more as being one of the early developers of the scientific method (often credited to Francis Bacon, some 500 years later)—with his strong emphasis on experimental verification of any result or supposition. Ibn al-Haytham is also widely regarded as the early 'father of optics', with his *Kitab*

---

[12] Al-Khwarizmi, *The Algebra of Mohammad ben Musa,* Hildesheim, Germany: George Olms Verlag, 1986, p. 3. Translated and edited by Frederic Rosen.

[13] Ibn Abi Usaybi`a, in his `*Uyun al-anba' fi tabaqat al-atibba'*, mentions that the famous caliph Umar ibn Abd al-`Aziz found an important Greek medical treatise (known by its Arabic title, '*al-Kunnash*') that had been translated from Syriac into Arabic, and deemed it so essential that he ordered that it be duplicated and made easily accessible to the general public.

al-Manadhir (Book of Optics, ca. 1000), where he not only showed unequivocally that vision proceeded with light entering the eye (and not being emitted by it), giving a full physical and physiological account of the process of vision, but also presented numerous optical instruments (mirrors of various shapes) and phenomena, including reflection and refraction.

Perhaps the field of the greatest and longest activity of this scientific golden age was Islamic Astronomy (often mixed with Astrology). Most notably, the Islamic civilisation is to be credited with erecting remarkable astronomical observatories, spanning 8 centuries and many lands, from Turkey to India, including Maragha (in today's western Iran), where an observatory that lasted only 30 years produced the greatest school of astronomy of that era, and Samarqand, where one instrument on the ground had a radius of 40 meters. Illustrious Muslim astronomers of that period include Al-Battani (d. 929), Al-Biruni (973–1048), Ibn Yunus (d. 1009), Al-Majriti (d. ca. 1007), As-Sufi (903–986), Az-Zarqali (ca. 1029–ca.1080), Al-Tusi (1201–1274), Ibn al-Shatir (1304–1375), Al-Qushji (1403–1474), Al-Khafri (ca. 1470-1550), and Taqi al-Din (16th c.).

Another area of the great Muslim scientific contribution was medicine, which was turned into an experimental science by people like the polymath Ibn Sina (980–1037), who was the first to conduct clinical trials. This great man is also credited with the discovery of the contagious nature of infectious diseases and the early development of clinical pharmacology. His *Al-Qanun fi-l-tibb* (The Canon in Medicine) remained the standard textbook in Europe until the 18th century! Other important contributors to medicine during the Islamic golden age include: Al-Razi (d. 923–24), who applied his chemical knowledge to medicine; al-Zahrawi (d. ca. 1013), famous for the surgical tools he used and described in his great work, *al-Tasrif* (*Vade Mecum*), a medical encyclopaedia in 30 sections, which also described interesting methods of preparing drugs by sublimation and distillation.[14] Also, Ibn al-Baytar (ca.

---

[14] Ead, Hamed A. 2004. *"History of Islamic Science, based on the book Introduction to the History of Science by George Sarton."* http://omaribnalkhatab.org/Cul-

1188–1248), an Andalusian botanist, pharmacist, and physician, whose most important contribution is *Al-Kitab Al-Jami` li-Mufradat al-Adwiya wa al-Aghdhiya (Compendium on Simple Medicaments and Foods)*, which not only referenced 150 previous Arab authors and 20 Greek authors, but listed 1,400 plants, foods, and drugs. His second major work is *Al-Kitab al-Mughni fi al-Adwiya al-Mufradaa (The Sufficient Book on Simple Drugs)*, an encyclopaedia of Islamic medicine, incorporating knowledge of plants into the treatment of various ailments of the head, ear, eye, etc.

Science in the Islamic world began to decline around the 12th century. Scientific achievements reached a high peak in the 10th–11th century and decreased to a very low level of activity by the 16th century and beyond. Toby Huff, for example, places the beginning of the decline around the late-thirteenth/early-fourteenth century (Huff, 1993), and David Lindbergh states that "by the fifteenth century, little was left" (Lindbergh 1992). Several factors contributed to the decline, some external (the Christian Crusades and Reconquista and the Mongol invasions, when libraries, observatories, hospitals, and schools were destroyed; the rise of Europe in the 15th century; and the economic decline of the Islamic states) and some internal (the rise of the orthodox theology after Ghazzali, the lack of institutionalisation of the culture of science, the absence of real universities or institutions of higher education with an autonomous status, the social chasm between the elite and the lay culture, etc.)

By the 12th century, Europe had begun to revitalize its culture with the (hugely impactful) creation of universities (Bologna, Paris, Oxford, and others) where a liberal curriculum was gradually constructed and a spirit of investigation and questioning was nurtured toward the entire corpus of human knowledge. This was no doubt strongly aided by the intellectual treasures obtained through contacts with the Muslim civilisation (particularly in Spain and Sicily) and the wide movement of translation of Greek and Islamic texts of philosophy and science from Arabic to Latin. Travels to faraway

ture/History%20Science.htm

lands (India and China in particular) also brought in additional knowledge which was used as a foundation for further development.

By the 13th century, early forms of the scientific method, and an understanding of the need to describe phenomena and results mathematically, were beginning to take root in Europe, with the works of scholars such as Robert Grosseteste (1175–1253) and Roger Bacon (1214–1292), paving the way to Copernicus and Galileo…

Modern Science (Mid-16thc. – Present)

The newly established European universities, with their curriculum of open studies and reviews of philosophy and science, along with theology and the arts, bore fruits that changed the course of human history. The Renaissance, the Scientific Revolution, the Enlightenment, and later the Industrial Revolution; all can be traced back to that educational and intellectual transformation.

The Scientific Revolution is widely considered to have started in 1543 when Copernicus published his paradigm-shifting book *De Revolutionibus* (how planets revolve [around the sun]), in which he argued on theoretical and observational grounds that the sun must be the centre of the 'world' (heliocentrism) and not the earth (geocentrism). In doing so, he made the earth a mere planet, and humans were no longer the centre of the universe. What he presented to be a 'small shift' in the position of the earth was in fact a huge scientific, intellectual and even theological earthquake.

The Scientific Revolution, which ushered in the era of Modern Astronomy, and later Modern Science as a whole, encompassed other groundbreaking contributions by Kepler, Galileo, and Newton who, with his *Principia*, made physics firmly mathematical (with the introduction of calculus), unified celestial laws with earthly physical laws, and changed the nature of science from its medieval approach to a new modern outlook.

Kepler (between 1609 and 1618) eliminated the centuries-old circles that made up planetary orbits and replaced them with ellipses. Galileo turned the study of motion (kinematics) into a precise mathematical science and, more importantly, introduced the telescope to astronomy, thereby changing our view of the heavens and making discoveries (Jupiter's moons, but most particularly the succession of the phases of Venus) which confirmed Copernicus's heliocentric thesis. This led to his famous prosecution by the Vatican, for religious/philosophical reasons, resulting in house arrest for the rest of his life, which did not prevent him from writing some of his most influential books. Kepler's laws of planetary motion later allowed Newton to construct his laws of motion and his universal law of gravity—the discovery that the way the earth attracts the moon and makes it revolve around it or the sun does with the earth and other planets is also the way objects on earth fall from trees. Kepler also invented a new telescope, much better than the one that Galileo developed, which in turn was based on an original Dutch design.

There were many significant contributors to the new age of science and reason, including Tycho Brahe, Robert Hooke, Christiaan Huygens, Gottfried Leibniz, and Rene Descartes, a period which continued into the 18th century.

The 17th century witnessed the important institutionalisation of science with the creation of academies of science, bodies of scientific scholars of the highest level providing a forum for the discussion of new ideas. The first and perhaps the most famous one is the Royal Society of London for Improving Natural Knowledge, more commonly known as 'the Royal Society', which was founded in 1660. It was there that Newton, Darwin and other illustrious scientists presented their works and held serious debates. The French Académie des Sciences was created in 1666. Others followed in the 18th and 19th centuries: the Norwegian Academy of Science and Letters was established in 1760, the Academy of Sciences of Lisbon, Portugal in 1779, the US National Academy of Sciences in 1863, and so on.

The 19th century also saw the professionalisation of science, i.e. the appearance of 'scientists', people whose careers and lives were devoted to scientific research. In those times, physics focused on the study of electricity and magnetism, with seminal discoveries by Faraday, Ohm, and others, which culminated with Maxwell's theoretical unification of the two phenomena as 'electromagnetism' under 'Maxwell's equations'.

An even greater scientific revolution occurred in the 19th century with discoveries and new theories in Biology. The most famous name associated with that revolution is certainly Charles Darwin, but other groundbreaking discoveries were made by Theodor Schwann and Matthias Schleiden and by Louis Pasteur and Robert Koch.

Until Darwin, biological studies were essentially taxonomies in botany and zoology, where organisms (plants or animals) were ordered in a system of species, genus, family, order and class, etc. The Swedish naturalism Carl von Linné had introduced a simple but rather artificial classification system that was based on a few key features, but it cried for a more natural and underlying relational scheme.

The idea of the evolution of species, with features and characteristics changing over short or long periods of time, had been discussed since antiquity, but first there were only vague explanations to those changes ("the environment forces those changes"), and secondly it wasn't clear that species changed overall and produced new ones. In France, Lamarck (1744 –1829) suggested that species do change over time, proposing that changes in an environment (long droughts or cold spells) produce changes in some species to enable them to adapt, and some of those changes can be radical enough to produce a new species.

In 1831, Darwin embarked on a historic journey onboard the Beagle ship, which took him around the world (in five years) and allowed him to observe countless creatures and take hundreds of pages of notes on their features and differences from place to place. The journey also allowed him to witness the effects of earthquakes and other natural drivers on various organisms and their ecosystems. That wealth of information, along with—upon his return to England—his reading of Malthus's 'An Essay on the Principle of Population', allowed him to make his historic breakthrough: species evolve gradually due to changes that occur in them naturally, with the environment selecting and preserving the ones that fit the physical conditions. He put his idea aside for a while, but when he received a paper from Alfred Russel Wallace showing that the latter had essentially arrived at the same discovery, he rushed to write his famous book, *On the Origin of Species,*[15] showing not only that he had made the same discovery earlier than Wallace but that he had a wealth of data to support it. Graciously, he read Wallace's paper along with a summary of his work together at the Linnaean Society in London on 1st July 1858; he followed this up with the publication of his book in 1859.

Two other momentous breakthroughs in Biology were made in the 19th century: the formulation of the cell theory (cells are the basic units of life, from bacteria of complex organs in living organisms)[16] by Theodor Schwann and Matthias Schleiden in 1838. This was made possible by the great improvements made to microscopes in the 18th and early 19th centuries and the formulation of the germ theory of diseases by Pasteur in France and Koch in Germany, who showed that many diseases were caused by bacterial infections of organisms, which then allowed for the development of treatment methods based on immunology.

In the 20th century, physics came back to the fore with several stunning revolutions. Albert Einstein burst on the scene in 1905 with several groundbreaking papers, introducing the hugely transformative theory of relativity and participating in the quantum

---

[15] The full title of Darwin's book was *On the Origin of Species by Means of Natural Selection, or the Preservation of Favoured Races in the Struggle for Life.*

[16] It was Robert Hooke who, in the 17th century, first observed 'cells' in wood layers through the newly invented microscope, gave detailed descriptions of the cells, and gave them that name, as they looked like prison cells to him...

revolution that Max Planck had started in 1900. Niels Bohr, Werner Heisenberg, Erwin Schrodinger, and others completed the quantum theory, which opened so many fields in novel ways, from atomic and nuclear physics to nanoscience and even biology. Einstein followed up his single-handed shake-up of physics in 1905 with another master work in 1915, his theory of general relativity, which allowed cosmology to take off from solid theoretical grounds as well as large-scale astrophysics (galaxies, quasars, black holes and other objects and phenomena).

Georges Lemaitre, George Gamow and others introduced the Big Bang theory, allowing humans to finally construct a 'big history' from the moment of creation to the present time, with different branches of science coming together in one epic story. It covers: particle and radiation physics during the big bang; general relativity during the following era of expansion and formation of galaxies; gravity, nuclear physics, and radiation during the formation of stars and planets, our solar system in particular; thermal and geological processes in the early phase of earth; the appearance of water, CO_2, life, and oxygen in the next phase of our planet; biology in the next stage, with the evolution of life and complex organisms; advanced evolution with the appearance of animals and then humans; and finally a cultural, scientific, and technological era when humans start to understand this cosmic and biological history and to explore the universe.

The 21st century promises more such great explorations, discoveries and leaps in knowledge, with our attempts to find other earths, to understand the early history of the universe with more accuracy and detail and to explore the smallest scale of the nano-world and of biology (in genetic engineering and other such fields).

The grand adventure continues…

CHAPTER 3

What is Modern Science?
And Why Do Some Thinkers Criticise It?

"What do you think science is? There's nothing magical about science. It is simply a systematic way for carefully and thoroughly observing nature and using consistent logic to evaluate results. Which part of that exactly do you disagree with? Do you disagree with being thorough? Using careful observation? Being systematic? Or using consistent logic?"

— Steven Novella

The Definition and Characteristics of Modern Science

IN OUR BRIEF HISTORICAL REVIEW of the evolution of science, we noted how in the last few centuries science underwent several highly important developments. Firstly, an empirical basis, whereby phenomena are investigated observationally and experimentally and rigorously as possible. Secondly, a strong mathematical basis, with physical laws in particular being expressed as mathematical formulas. Thirdly, a professionalisation and institutionalisation of scientific activity, with full-fledged 'scientists' appearing in various places, universities teaching well-tuned curricula, and academies of science providing a forum for discoveries and proposed ideas to be shared and discussed. And finally, the emergence of a 'philosophy of science' that attempts to put science and its methodology on firm grounds and filter out 'pseudo-science' and 'non-science'.

With the Copernicus-Kepler-Galileo-Newton revolution we could, from the 17th century onward, speak of Modern Astronomy. Also, from the 19th century, with the revolutions made by Darwin, Maxwell,

Einstein, Heisenberg, Schrodinger, Lemaitre and Hubble, we could speak of Modern Science (Modern Biology, Modern Physics, Modern Cosmology, etc.).

The aforementioned characteristics of Modern Science are important to understand, for several reasons: a) as noted above, it is essential to differentiate between what is truly a scientific topic and investigation from what is 'pseudo-science' (e.g. astrology); b) understanding the nature of Modern Science will allow us to construct a rational, reasonable and acceptable relation between it and religion/Islam.

Modern science can generally be defined as: "an organised, systematic and disciplined mode of inquiry based on experimentation and empiricism that produces repeatable and applicable results universally, across all cultures."[17] This definition has the virtue of emphasising the characteristics of objectivity (repeatability, universality) and testability (experimentation, empiricism). It further refers indirectly to the *process* of Science (the 'scientific method'), and incorporates Karl Popper's 'falsifiability' criterion ('testability'), which declares as non-scientific any proposed explanation that cannot be checked, with the aim of either confirming it or rejecting it as incorrect. This is important as it allows for a distinction between science and other great fields of human knowledge or activity e.g. art, philosophy, religion and more.

This definition, however, does not mention, at least not explicitly, what in my view is the fundamental characteristic of modern science—namely the principle of 'methodological naturalism'. This insists that science only admits explanations of natural phenomena that rely solely on natural causes and leave out entirely any appeal to supernatural agents, be they spirits, angels, demons, or God Himself. It is important to stress right away that Modern Science does not reject the concept of God or anyone's belief in Him or other supernatural agents; it only insists that scientific explanations of natural

---

[17] Sardar, Z. (2006), "Islamic science: the way ahead", in E. Masood (Ed.), *How do you know?*, London: Pluto Press, p. 181.

phenomena be based on natural causes. This is simply a pragmatic, neutral, and constructive stance: first, scientists note that we have made much greater progress when we looked for natural explanations of phenomena (from lightning and earthquakes to epilepsy and schizophrenia) than when we assumed they were produced by God or demons. Secondly, with the diversity of cultures in the world, the only things we can agree on are the facts of nature we all observe in the same way. If we were to admit other non-scientific assumptions/explanations then each of us might have his/her biased cultural beliefs and 'explanations' for this or that phenomenon.

This framework of Modern Science has posed a challenge to at least some Islamic conceptions of the world and nature, as often Muslims claim and insist that God acts physically and directly in the world, in cases of miracles or in everyday events, either at a large scale (earthquakes, floods, etc.) or small, individual, personal scales (in responses to prayers, in particular). However, one must recall that this issue had been raised and debated by Muslim theologians in the past, with discussions of 'secondary causes'. Indeed, God being the primary cause for everything, the debate between philosophers and theologians (Mu`tazilites and Ash`aris) was whether phenomena in nature followed laws and 'secondary causes' or whether God had to be invoked in each and every instant for every atom, cell and ray or light.

Illustrious Muslim scientists of the golden age, particularly Ibn Al-Haytham (965–1040) and Al-Biruni (973–1048), insisted on natural explanations for the phenomena they were attempting to explain. The Mu`tazilites, chiefly represented by the great theologian Qadi `Abd al-Jabbar (d. ca. 1024) held the view that God operates according to rational laws.[18] The Ash`aris, however, who to this day are the largely dominant theological school in the Muslim world, insist that God holds every process, small or large, and acts at every instant. Muslims who are more in line with the modern scientific approach see no contradiction in believing that God 'sustains' the

---

[18] Campanini, M. (2005), "Qur'an and science: A hermeneutical approach", *Journal of Qur'anic Studies, 7*(1), 54-55.

world through the laws that he has put in nature, and that natural causes are indirectly God allowed causes.

The Scientific Method

We often represent the 'basic' scientific method as a simple series of procedures: 1) observations of a phenomenon; 2) formulation of a hypothesis to explain it; 3) making predictions from that hypothesis to test it; 4) testing the hypothesis by performing experiments or observations; 5) confirming or rejecting the hypothesis, in which case the cycle is repeated.

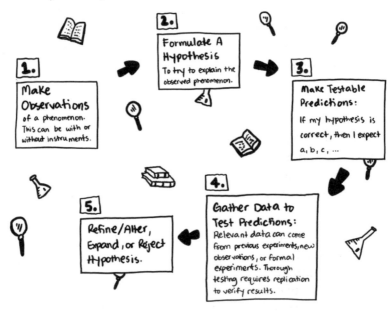

Figure 3 – *The Scientific Method as an ongoing process.*[19]

The formulation of this 'standard' scientific method is often credited to Francis Bacon (1561–1626), **not** because he was actually the first to implement it, but because he seems to have been the first to clearly describe it. Indeed, we know that scientists from earlier ep-

---

[19]   https://commons.wikimedia.org/wiki/File:The_Scientific_Method_as_an_Ongoing_Process.svg

ochs, particularly Ibn al-Haytham, had adopted and implemented a strongly empirical and experimental approach.

In fact, some philosophers of science, most famously Paul Feyerabend (1924–1994) and Imre Lakatos (1922–1974), debated whether science had a method that could be clearly defined and, more importantly, whether it could at all be described as objective. This question's relevance is clear when one considers that scientists are human and thus subject to hidden inclinations and prone to human error.

In practice, however, scientists follow the scientific method only broadly, for two reasons: a) there is obviously some overlap between several of the 'steps' in this method, for example that hypotheses and tests are intertwined and influence each other; b) scientists can come up with hypotheses from any source, even dreams, not necessarily from direct empirical activity.

Scientific Hypotheses, Facts, Laws, Models and Theories

It helps immensely to understand what science is saying if one can clearly distinguish between some fundamental terms, the following in particular: fact, law, hypothesis, model and theory. Below I will try to define each term as simply and as clearly as possible:

- **A scientific fact** may simply be defined as an objective and verifiable observation: 'objective' means that it is independent of the observer, anyone who repeats the act is the same conditions will obtain the same results. There are numerous examples of scientific facts nowadays, from the most well-known: Earth is round, rotates around itself, and revolves around the sun—no matter what flat-earthers and other deniers of a heliocentric solar system say, to the most contentious: Earth is 4.5 billion years old, and there is observed evidence of biological evolution in the Earth's geological and paleontological record, many asserting that they rise to the level of facts.

- **A scientific law** is a formulation (often mathematical) of a causal relationship between physical quantities that has been found to always hold. For example, Newton's first law: "in the absence of a net force, an object will remain either at rest or in uniform motion (depending on its current state of motion)". Other examples of important laws are given in the next few pages.

- **A hypothesis** is a proposition that a scientist formulates as a possible explanation of a given observation or phenomenon. For example: "the sky is blue because the sky reflects the blue colour of the waters on Earth." This is not only a plausible hypothesis, it is a valid, scientific one, because it proposes an explanation for an observed phenomenon (the sky is blue) and it is 'falsifiable', i.e. one can test it and find out if it is correct or not (by watching the sky from the desert or any place devoid of waters). Indeed, as one can see from this example, a hypothesis is not always correct; in fact, incorrect hypotheses have been formulated dozens or hundreds of times more often than correct ones.

- **A model** is a reduced version of a physical system and its processes as envisioned by a scientist, simplified enough that it allows the scientist to study it and its main factors, but not overly simplified such that it stops representing reality correctly. For example, the atom was originally represented as a little spherical nucleus around which electrons orbited. It was soon realised that such a 'planetary model' could not represent an atom correctly, because first of all, an electron (and all electric charges) that is subjected to acceleration will radiate, thus lose energy rather quickly and fall on the nucleus. The quantum 'cloud' model was then proposed to replace the 'planetary model'.

- **A scientific theory** is produced when scientists synthesise a body of evidence or observations of particular phenomena with the laws that have been found to be true, and the mathematical relations that connect things together. Sometimes a theory can be summarised in one or a few statement(s) or equation(s), sometimes it is a more complex body of laws and observed facts. Some examples include: Newton's gravitational theory; Einstein's relativity theories; the quantum theory of atoms and particles; Maxwell's equations of electromagnetism, the tectonic-plate theory, the theory of evolution and several others and many more.

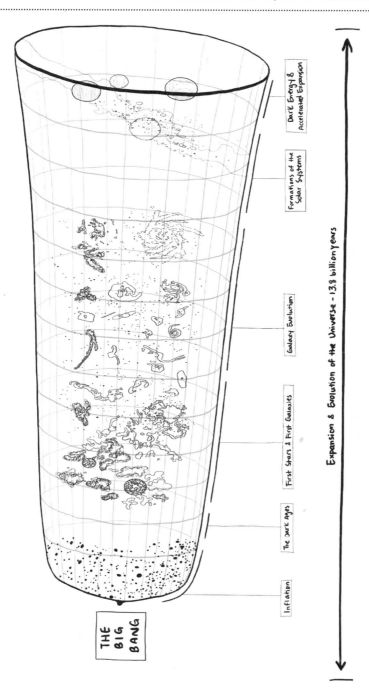

Dark Energy & Accelerated Expansion

Formations of the Solar Systems

Galaxy Evolution

First Stars & First Galaxies

The Dark Ages

Inflation

Expansion & Evolution of the Universe - 13.8 billion years

THE BIG BANG

Figure 4a – *Scientific theories: the Big Bang.*

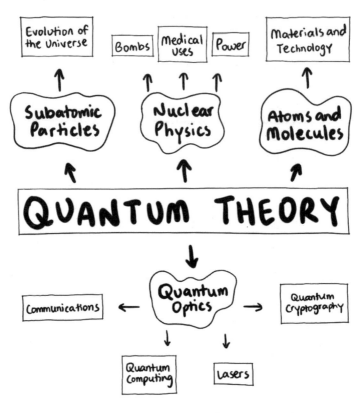

Figure 4b – *Scientific theories: the Quantum Theory.*

I like to use a simple analogy to illustrate the concepts of 'facts', 'laws' and theories: the example of a house. A house is made of solid bricks (those are the 'facts'); they are glued together by logic and math; the columns and beams represent the 'laws' that relate those 'facts'; the entire frame of the house, with its roof, windows, doors, balconies and other such elements represent the 'theory'.

> *"Science is facts. Just as houses are made of stones, so is science made of facts. But a pile of stones is not a house and a collection of facts is not necessarily science."*
>
> *– Henri Poincaré*

As to scientific laws, some of the most important ones that people are generally familiar with include:

- **Newton's "Universal Law of Gravitation":** Somewhat 350 years ago, Isaac Newton proposed the (then revolutionary) idea that any two objects, no matter how large and how far apart they may be, whether here on Earth or in the cosmos (hence 'universal law'), attract each other with a gravitational force that is given by a simple formula that all students learn in school today: $F = G \times M1M2/D^2$. F is the force, G is a universal constant $= 6.67 \times 10\text{-}11 \text{ N m}^2 \text{ kg}$, M1 and M2 are the masses of the two objects, and D is the distance between their two centres. The same force applies to the two objects, regardless of how small or large each one is. This same formula is also used today to describe most planetary and lunar orbits, as well as the satellites we place around Earth. It also allows us to determine the masses of objects (stars or planets) if we can measure the orbital parameters (distance and period) of objects that may orbit around them.

- **Newton also gave us 3 other famous laws**; his laws of motion, which together with his law of gravity form an essential part of classical physics, particularly mechanics. Like many scientific laws, they are beautiful in their simplicity. The first one, I mentioned earlier. The second one simply relates the net force applied on an object of mass M to the acceleration that results from the force: $F = Ma$. The third one is familiar to most people: for every action on an Object X there is an equal and opposite reaction from X on the Object Y that exerted the force on X (again, regardless of how small or large each one is). In other words, every object that is subjected to a force will push back with equal force.

- Another important set of laws are **the 3 Laws of Thermodynamics**, which constitute the fundamental basis of the study of how energy and heat work in a system, e.g. an engine, the interior of a star etc. The 3 laws can be expressed as follows: 1) conservation of energy for systems where heat plays an important role; unless the system is perfectly 'closed' (isolated from the rest of the universe), some heat will inevitably be lost to the outside world; 2) 'entropy', which is essentially a measure of the 'disorder' of a system, will always increase in any thermo-dynamic process; in other words, a system will not produce more order from disorder by any natural process; 3) At 'Absolute Zero' Kelvin (273.15 degrees Celsius below zero), the lowest temperature possible, entropy reaches its lowest possible value, and all particles stop moving. Reaching absolute zero is thus impossible, but by pumping energy out of a system experimental scientists have reached milli-Kelvin levels of temperature.

An important question is whether the laws that we formulate are real or only temporary human constructs. Don't scientific laws change through centuries? Indeed, Newton's law of gravitation was found to be inadequate for Mercury and in regions of 'strong gravity' and had to be replaced by Einstein's equations of General Relativity. Here, one must distinguish between the 'laws of science', i.e. what scientists formulate, and the (real) 'laws of nature' or the 'laws of God' (as believers prefer to call them). Indeed, what scientists discover or formulate, i.e. the 'facts of nature' or the 'laws of science', are only gradually and progressively approaching the *real* laws of nature (or of God) according to which nature actually functions.

Are those 'laws of nature' fixed in time and space, or do they change? Muzaffar Iqbal[20] has stressed that "God's ways and laws are unchanging," citing the Qur'anic verse, "*That was the way of Allah in the case of those who passed away of old, and you will not find for the way of Allah any changes*" (33:62), and added: "thus the entire world of nature operates through immutable laws that can be discovered through the investigation of nature." Some scientists have suggested that the laws of the universe might actually have evolved; they have proposed tests for this hypothesis, but until now no observation or experiment has given any credence to that suggestion.

The Construction of Models and Laws—in Practice

Science relies heavily on modelling,[21] because it is often impossible to experiment on or mathematically represent the whole sys-

---

[20] Iqbal, M. (2007), *Science and Islam*, Westwood, CT: Greenwood Press, p. 6.

[21] Roman Frigg and Stephan Hartmann, "Models in Science", Stanford Encyclopaedia of Philosophy, 2012: http://plato.stanford.edu/entries/models-science/, retrieved 19 March, 2013.

tem under investigation—there are too many atoms in any piece of matter, there are too many interactions between the different parts of the system, it is too complex, etc. Thus science adopts various types of models, which can be physical objects (e.g. scaled-down versions of the problem), analogical models, numerical models, idealised systems and so forth. Some of the most iconic examples of models in science include: Bohr's planetary model of the atom, the double-helix model of the DNA molecule, the billiard-ball model of gases, the liquid-drop model and the shell model of the nucleus, the shell-structure model of Earth and many others.

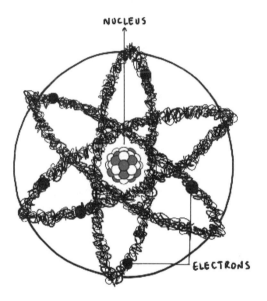

Figures 5a and 5b – *Scientific models: a) the 'planetary' atom; b) the Earth's structure.*

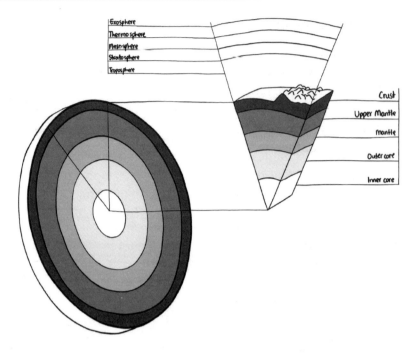

How does a model work? Firstly, a model is by nature a simplified version of the real system, one where the fundamental aspects are preserved, but the non-essential components have been left aside. This simplification, or idealisation, of the problem was introduced by Galileo (objects become point masses, surfaces become friction-less planes, etc.), and it has been formalised since then. Attention must be drawn to the risk of over-simplification or deletion of a crucial aspect of the problem. One must also have a rigorous understanding of the limits of accuracy of each model, depending on its characteristics. For instance, a numerical model will be more or less accurate depending on how linear or non-linear ('chaotic') the system is and on the time scales over which the computations are carried out. This is most famously manifested in weather-prediction models and in climate-change or global-warming models. Indeed, an important part of today's debates among scientists about how much one should trust global-warming predictions revolves around the model(s) being assumed (what effects have been included and how) and the accuracy of the numerical calculations.

Important Concepts for Today's Scientific Knowledge

In addition to the fundamental notions outlined above (facts, hypotheses, laws, theories or models), there are two additional important concepts that I would like to briefly outline, as they are very useful in understanding scientific information and in preventing us from drawing erroneous conclusions from results that are found or reported here or there.

1) Correlations

Correlations are relationships or connections between two or more quantities. Correlations can be 'positive' (when the two factors increase or decrease together) or 'negative' (when the two quantities vary in opposite ways). For example: students' grades increase with their class attendance (positive correlation); the amount of hair on people's heads decreases with their age (negative correlation); blood pressure increases with people's age (negative correlation); age expectancy decreases with more smoking in a population (negative correlation).

A very crucial note to make is that **correlation does not imply causation**, and this is a major source of erroneous conclusions by many people. A correlation between two quantities i.e. A and B could be due to a third factor C influencing both, so there could be causation between C and A and between C and B but not between A and B. Here are a few examples from the world around us to illustrate this important principle:

- One may note a correlation between the number of homeless people and the crime rate in a city. However, homelessness is not necessarily the cause for the higher crime rate. The two could be due to a high unemployment rate in that city or possibly additional factors, e.g. drug use (there are sometimes several causal factors in such correlations).

- One may note a correlation between the number of firemen present at a fire disaster and the amount of damage that is occurring, but obviously the first one is not causing the second.

- Likewise, one may note that children who are receiving tutoring lessons in a given subject tend to get lower grades than their classmates. Needless to say, the tutoring is not resulting in lower grades...

- There are a number of examples about correlations that occur in the summer; for instance, if one looks at the numbers of drownings and the sales of ice cream, one finds them increasing and decreasing at the same time, but obviously both are caused by the summer season which sends people both swimming and buying ice cream.

- Finally, a funny cartoon once had a child noting that, "Every time the captain turns on the 'Seatbelts On' sign, it gets bumpy..."

2) **Statistical significance**

One must be careful, when reading results of measurements, in deciding whether the effect that is being reported is 'significant' or not. Indeed, one must always remember that measurements come with errors (due to instruments, human mistakes or normal fluctuations), also called 'uncertainties', and every measurement must always be read with its error when compared with another value.

For example, if a new measurement gives $A = 4.7$, whereas a previous one gave 5.2, we must not jump to claim a significant difference (of about 10%), much less an inconsistency between the two, because that depends on the error or uncertainty over each of the two values. If both have an uncertainty of 0.3, then they are perfectly consistent, as 4.7 + 0.3 brings it within the range of the other (5.2 − 0.3 to 5.2 + 0.3). If the error was only 0.2, then the difference between the two measurements is indeed significant, and we can claim an inconsistency or a significant change in the value of that quantity – to a certain extent. I say "to a certain extent" because even then, the science of statistics tells us that there is a probability (roughly 5% or so) that even though the values of the two measurements (4.7 − 0.2 to 4.7 + 0.2) and (5.3 − 0.2 to 5.3 + 0.2) do not overlap, they do overlap if we take twice the uncertainty. Note that the probability for that is 5%, which is not small at all! What we can see from this illustration is that even measurements and results that appear to provide a certain conclusion must be subjected to rigorous scrutiny through the microscope of statistics to ensure their significance.

Modern Critiques of Science

Science has always had its critics both for objective (methodological) reasons and for other reasons (e.g. ideological). Most recently, new critiques have appeared, including religious (fundamentalist) and post-modern ones. Both of these claim that science, like other human endeavours, is a 'construct' that is no less subjective and ideological than other fields. Other critiques, e.g. the feminist one, claim that not only has the scientific enterprise been socially and culturally biased (toward western, male, privileged scientists), some of its conclusions might well have been different if the minds that produced them had been female or non-western. This view may seem surprising or even outlandish, but serious claims have been made to this effect, mostly in the social sciences. There have also been Islamic critiques of modern science which we shall review shortly.

Defenders of science, however, argue simply that the great successes of science over the past few centuries (countless confirmed predictions, life and society-transforming applications, etc. speak for themselves. While it is true that some sharpening of the methods, and probably some rectification of the sociology of the enterprise, could benefit science in certain fields, a general critique and devaluation of science is far from warranted.

An objective and perceptive assessment, however, leads one to acknowledge and highlight some important areas of substantial debate regarding modern science and how it functions. One such issue is 'reductionism', which is a general principle or methodology whereby the exploration of a subject or body is thought to be best done by breaking it into its different parts, understanding and analysing each aspect with its relation to the other parts, then re-constructing the body or the subject bottom up. This has worked very well in a number of areas, particularly in physics and chemistry, and also to some extent in biology, for example with the possible reduction of cell mechanisms to the chemical interaction of its parts.

However, the reductionist process becomes less and less straight-forward as one climbs the ladder of complexity, although, 'greedy reductionists' wish to keep applying the principle upward: psychology is presented as (at least in principle) a result of biology, consciousness is 'nothing but' a complex manifestation of brain processes and so on. This 'nothing-buttery' is often seen as a manifestation of an ideological, materialist agenda: if everything can be reduced to atoms and interactions, then we will not ever need to refer to the mind, much less to the soul. This has led contemporary philosophers like Fraser Watts to insist on distinguishing between 'methodological reductionism' and 'ideological reductionism'. In fact, scientists do know that many phenomena are not amenable to reductionist approaches, as indeed many 'emergent' phenomena (where at higher levels of complexity new phenomena appear that could never exist at lower levels), have been fully documented and studied.

Another area of general contention is the attempt by science to occupy as large (and unbounded) a space of investigation as possible, including human life and society. This is generally labelled as 'scientism' (a rather pejorative term). Indeed, while reductionism may not apply in many fields and phenomena, this does not imply that even something like consciousness could not, sooner or later, be fully explained by science. It is when we step into areas of human behaviour and endeavour, however, including psychological phenomena like love and spirituality, or social phenomena like religion, that the question of the relevance and capability of science becomes strongly contentious. Nomanul Haq[22] explains our tendency for scientism by the propensity of human societies to place scientists on a pedestal, thereby implying that they possess deeper

---

[22] S. Nomanul Haq, "Science, scientism, and the liberal arts", *Islam & Science*, December 2003.

understanding and comprehension of the world and thus should be entrusted with all our issues to address.

Islamic Thinkers' Views on Modern Science and its Methodology

The most famous Muslim critic of modern science is undoubtedly Seyyed Hossein Nasr, one of the most important Muslim philosophers of the past 50 years, with dozens of books, hundreds of articles and high honours.[23] His chief objection[24] is that modern science has adopted a naturalistic approach (keeping out all supernatural and spiritual agents) and thus denied any link to the divine, a link which he presents as essential. Another important and general objection[25] of Nasr is that modern science has fragmented and debased humans and corrupted nature, which he regards as sacred in Islam. Last but not least, he rejects some essential approaches of modern science (confirmation by repeatability, accuracy, etc.), as he places more importance in the values of purpose, meaning, beauty, harmony, etc.

In a similar fashion, the Muslim traditionalist thinker William Chittick dismisses the claim of objectivity of modern science, which he considers as essentially "a vast structure of beliefs and presuppositions."[26] He insists that "modern scientists, intellectuals and scholars have acquired all their knowledge by imitation, not realisation. They take what they call 'facts' from others, without verifying their truth..." As we have explained above, this accusation is baseless; on

---

[23] Nasr is only one of two Muslim philosophers to have so far given the famous and prestigious Gifford Lectures; he was also included in the Library of Living Philosophers; etc.

[24] Seyyed Hossein Nasr, "Islam and the Problem of Modern Science," in Ziauddin Sardar (ed.), "*An Early Crescent: The Future of Knowledge and the Environment*", Mansell, London, 1989, p. 132.

[25] Ibrahim Kalin, "The Sacred versus the Secular: Nasr on Science", in "Library of living philosophers: Seyyed Hossein Nasr", L. E. Hahn, R. E. Auxier and L. W. Stone (eds.), Open Court Press, Chicago, 2001, pp. 445–462.

[26] William Chittick, "*Science of the Cosmos, Science of the Soul: The Pertinence of Islamic Cosmology in the Modern World*", Oneworld, Oxford (UK), 2007, p. 24.

the contrary, modern science insists on objectivity (independence from the scientist who proposes any model or reports any result), prediction and testing, and falsifiability of any hypothesis. No results are ever taken "without verifying their truths..."

Other Muslim thinkers have disagreed with Nasr and Chittick's overly negative assessment and rejection of modern science and its methods, particularly Ziauddin Sardar[27] and Mohammad Hashim Kamali,[28] even though both Sardar and Kamali have their own minor quarrels with science. Kamali makes two important points: 1) Islam (through a number of hadiths, i.e. Prophetic statements or actions) teaches us to welcome knowledge produced by other peoples, even if that knowledge is not 'rooted in God' or aimed at leading to Him; in fact, Kamali does not see a fundamental difference between the goals of modern science and those of Islam as both are concerned with seeking truths; 2) the Qur'an brings forth a certain philosophy of knowledge/science, and in several verses one finds it supporting a methodology of observation and experimentation as well as inductivism (e.g. Q 22:46).[29] Indeed, Kamali recalls that Mohammad Iqbal (the great Indian thinker of the early 20th century) saw the Qur'an as "the birth of the 'inductive intellect'" and considers it "a religious obligation, therefore, of every Muslim to master the inductive method..."

Conclusion

> *"Science is a way of thinking much more than it is a body of knowledge."*
> *–Carl Sagan*

It is important for Muslims (and of course all other humans) to fully understand how modern science works, what are its basic methods, and where its boundaries and limits lie, even though

---

[27] Ziauddin Sardar, "Explorations in Islamic Science", Mansell, London, 1989

[28] Mohammad Hashim Kamali, "Islam, Rationality, and Science", *Islam & Science*, Vol. 1 (June 2003) No. 1, pp. 115-134.

[29] "Do they not travel through the land, so that their hearts (and minds) may thus learn wisdom and their ears may thus learn to hear? For indeed it is not the eyes that grow blind, but the hearts, which are in the breasts." (Q 22:46)

there may be some disagreements on the latter. Most importantly, we must be clear about what areas are the purview of science, where religion must not interfere or claim any veto rights, and what areas are beyond science (e.g. love and spirituality). Though it can shed some light on how the human mind functions, how humans behave, what mistakes are often made in thinking about such topics, etc.

To sum up and further emphasise, the most important characteristics of modern science are: empiricism (everything must start with observations and measurements), objectivity (independence from any person, universal repeatability of the result), and testability (by experimentation) of any claim or hypothesis—what Popper has called 'falsifiability'—that no hypothesis can be considered scientific unless it presents predictions that can be tested for confirmation or rejection.

We have also seen how science is more a *process* (the 'scientific method', whether we consider it in its simplistic or more complex forms), than a body of knowledge. We have also stressed the fundamental distinctions required between facts and hypotheses, models, theories and laws.

Having established these important methodological clarifications, we are now ready to proceed (in the following/proceeding chapter) with what modern science has taught us so far and, in subsequent chapters we will discover what issues it may have raised for Islam and Muslims that we must, and can, address.

CHAPTER 4
··················
All the (Basic) Science that You Need to Know

"Curiosity—the rover [on Mars] and the concept—is what science is all about: the quest to reveal the unknown."

– Ahmed Zewail (Nobel Prize winner in Chemistry, 1999)

Introduction

AS WE LEARNED IN THE previous chapter, science is both methodology and knowledge of the world, knowledge made as certain as possible by that methodology. The methodology, as described earlier, consists of a series of steps by which scientific knowledge is built as well as steps by which claims are checked and information is ascertained.

In this chapter, I will present a summary of what we now know about the world, as well as all the essential scientific knowledge that any educated person should have today. This will later allow us to establish well-informed answers to arising issues at the science-religion interface.

For instance, in order to understand topics such as the Big Bang and the place of Earth in the universe, we will need to learn about matter and radiation, and the fundamental interactions between nuclei and atoms. In biology, before we get to evolution, we will need to learn about the DNA molecule, genes and chromosomes, cells, and some other key concepts and processes.

We will limit our review to Physics, Astronomy/Cosmology and Biology: the three essential fields of modern science, because of the major revolutions that they have undergone over the last century or so, and because they lead to topics that tend to raise religious issues. Indeed, before we can discuss any religious or philosophical implications of that knowledge, we will need a general overview of "all the (basic) science that you need to know".

Your Essential Physics

Nature can be divided simply into matter and radiation. Richard Feynman, one of the greatest physicists of the twentieth century, once stated[30] that the one sentence about science that would be most important to pass down to future generations is: "All things are made of atoms—little particles that move around in perpetual motion, attracting each other when they are a little distance apart, but repelling upon being squeezed into one another."

The atom is the basic building block of matter. The name comes from the Greek *atomos*, meaning indivisible, or smallest piece of matter (say carbon), but in fact atoms can be split, and they are indeed made of smaller 'particles': electrons and nuclei, the latter being made of protons and neutrons, which themselves are made of quarks, which are bound by gluons (see Figure 6).

However, a bunch of protons or neutrons or electrons do not make up any 'matter' until they are structured as atoms. And the way an atom is constructed is: 1 proton and 1 electron make a hydrogen atom; 2 protons, 1 or 2 neutrons, and 2 electrons make a helium atom and so forth. A simple and very useful way to represent and order the atomic elements, both those that exist naturally in the universe and those that we create temporarily in laboratories, is the famous 'periodic table', which was first constructed by Dmitri Mendeleev in 1869. Originally, it was ordered by 'atomic weight', from lightest to heaviest, but it was later realised that it should be ordered by the 'atomic number', i.e. by the number of electrons (or, equally, protons) in each atom/element, as the atomic number really determines the chemical properties of each element.

---

[30] http://www.feynmanlectures.caltech.edu/I_01.html#Ch1-S2

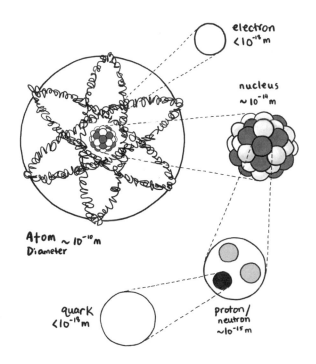

electron
$< 10^{-18}$ m

nucleus
$\sim 10^{-14}$ m

Atom $\sim 10^{-10}$ m
Diameter

quark
$< 10^{-18}$ m

proton/
neutron
$\sim 10^{-15}$ m

Figure 6 – *The particles that make up an atom and its nucleus.*

Atoms can combine into molecules, such as H_2O (water) or CO_2 (carbon dioxide), by having their external electrons 'bond' in various ways (see Figure 7). Depending on the temperature and pressure conditions, matter (e.g. water) can exist in various 'phases': gas, liquid, solid, or plasma (when some or all electrons have been removed from the atoms or molecules).

Furthermore, each element can exist as different isotopes, depending on how many neutrons there are in the nucleus. For example, 6 protons in a nucleus will automatically mean carbon, but depending on whether it has 6, 7, or 8 neutrons in its nucleus, the carbon will be of the 12, 13, or 14 type isotope, denoted ^{12}C, ^{13}C, ^{14}C.

Only certain isotopes are stable, others decay faster or slower. Carbon-14, for instance, has a 'half-life' of 5730 years (half of any amount will have decayed after that time, and then half of what

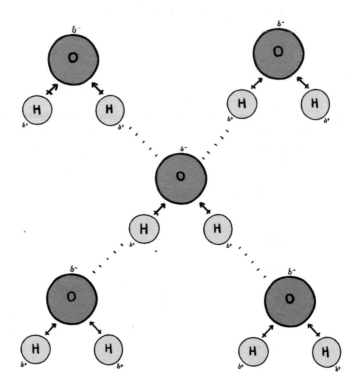

Figure 7 – *How the atoms bind in the water (H2O) molecule, and how the molecules weakly interact amongst themselves.*

remains will decay in another 5730 years, etc.), and this is actually very useful in allowing us to date organic material that goes back thousands of years. For example, the Turin Shroud, a piece of linen that was thought to be imprinted with the image of Jesus Christ (peace be upon him) was carbon-dated in 1988 by three separate laboratories and was found to go back to the 14th century, not to the time of Jesus Christ.

Other isotopes of lesser known elements are also unstable ('radio-active') and have much longer half-lives, millions or billions of years, thus allowing us to date bones or rocks that go back millions or billions of years in the past.

All elements up to number 83 (Bismuth) have at least one stable isotope. Heavier ones, such as Uranium (92) and Plutonium (94), have only unstable isotopes and are thus fully radioactive.

Reactions between nuclei can either fuse nuclei (if they are small/light) or split/fission them (if they are heavy); in both cases, relatively large amounts of energy are released. This is what humans do in nuclear weapons ('atomic bombs' use fission on Uranium or Plutonium, and 'hydrogen bombs' use fusion of isotopes of hydrogen) in very short but huge explosions, or more gradually using 'controlled fission' in nuclear power plants.

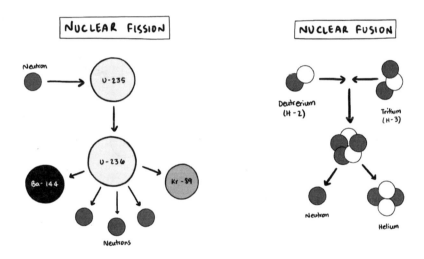

Figure 8 – *The nuclear fission and fusion processes.*

Nuclear fusion is in fact the most important energy source in the universe! Almost all energy in the universe comes from stars, and they all produce the energy that they shine through their surfaces by nuclear reactions that occur in their very hot and dense cores. There, mostly hydrogen, helium or carbon (in the late stages of stars) fuse together to form heavier nuclei, a process which releases tremendous amounts of energy. This is the same process that occurs in the short and huge explosions of hydrogen-bombs and in the process that we have been trying to master in 'fusion reactors', so far without great success. Nature is able to do it because stars are very large objects and their internal gravitational inward pressure is able to raise the temperature in the cores to tens or hundreds of millions of degrees, which then allows the nuclei to overcome their electric repulsion (being all positively charged, thus repelling each other) and come close enough for nuclear attraction to fuse them.

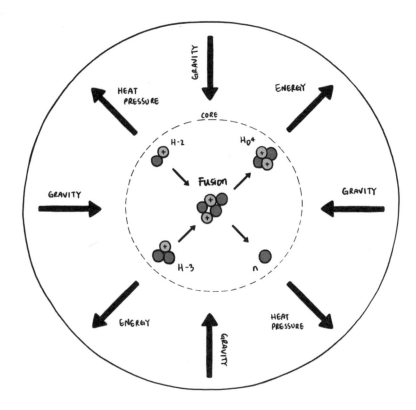

Figure 9 – *Nuclear energy production in the core of the Sun and equilibrium between gravitational (inward) and heat (outward) pressures.*

This is also the same process that occurred during the first three minutes of the Big Bang, during which protons fused into helium nuclei, and the latter produced small amounts of lithium and beryllium. Indeed, calculating how much of each could be produced in that way and comparing it with the amounts we find in the universe today is one of the main ways by which we can confirm that the Big Bang is a correct cosmological model of the early universe.

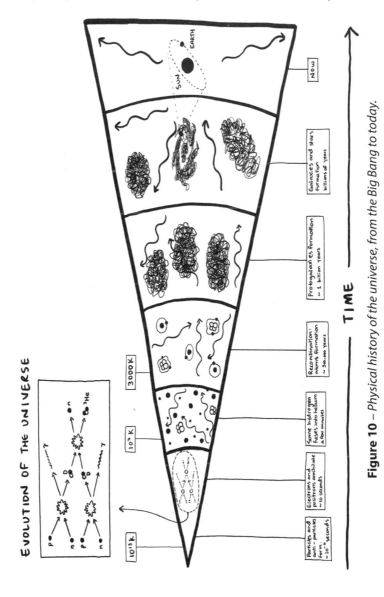

Figure 10 – *Physical history of the universe, from the Big Bang to today.*

Radiation has acquired a frightening connotation because it tends to be associated with dangers and weapons such as nuclear bombs and accidents. If our bodies are exposed to large doses of radioactivity, mutations and cancer are likely to occur. Indeed, in very large doses, radiation can be deadly, but most of the time it is rather harmless, and it is ubiquitous and needed in various areas of our lives.

There are essentially two types of radiation; one is associated with particles (alpha, which is helium nuclei, beta, which is electrons or anti-electrons, and protons and neutrons). The other is associated with electromagnetic (light) waves of various wavelengths, frequencies, and energies, from radio through visible light down to gamma rays, but particularly the 'higher end' of the spectrum, i.e. ultra-violet, x-rays and gamma rays.

The important distinction between the various types of radiation is usually based on its energy level. The strongest radiation is known as 'ionising', because it can create ions in the matter it penetrates, by removing electrons from atoms. This includes X-rays, gamma-rays and the particles that are emitted by the isotopes that decay (radioactively). Less powerful radiation is 'non-ionising'. In principle, ionising radiation is more dangerous to health than non-ionising radiation, but this also depends on the intensity of the source or the 'dose' that is received or absorbed by the recipient.

Einstein and Relativity

Albert Einstein and his relativity theory truly represent 20[th]century physics. Most people associate Einstein and Relativity with the formula $E = mc^2$ (energy and mass are equivalent and inter-related), but many people simplistically understand relativity to mean "motion is relative" or, worse, "all things are relative, depending on where you observe them from". In fact, Einstein's theory of (special) relativity, published in 1905, is based on two principles (assumptions that cannot be proven but lead to correct results): a) all physical phenomena must be describable in the same way (same equations) in reference frames that are either stationary or moving uniformly relative to one another, and b) the speed of light must have the same value, in all reference frames, if these move with respect to each other with constant velocity. In other words, if I am at rest, and you are moving uniformly (keeping the same speed and direction) with respect to me, then we must get the same value for the speed of light when we measure it (even though you are moving), and any phenomenon (e.g. projectile motion) must be describable in the same way (with the same equations) by each of us.

These simple principles lead to extraordinary consequences: contrary to our long-held conceptions, it turns out that time and space (position and distance) are not absolute but rather 'relative'. They combine and become a couple, space-time; they will each appear different (expand and contract) when measured in different reference frames—in order to keep the speed of light the same.

All this has not only been confirmed in laboratories, in a variety of experiments and for various effects; it has now become a feature of a number of applications, including GPS satellites, which depend on precise measurements of time in order to provide accurate map positions on Earth. The satellites are orbiting the planet at about 14,000 km/h, and if their clocks did not take into account relativistic effects on time, Google maps would be giving us positions that are 10 kilometres off within a day.[31]

Another result that emerges from the above relativistic considerations is the famous formula $E=mc^2$, where E is energy, m is mass and c is the speed of light. Energy and mass are thus equivalent and can be converted into one another, as happens in nuclear reactions, in stars and in atomic bombs, where the difference in mass between the initial and final nuclei is released as (lots of) energy (because c is high: 300,000 kilometres per second in vacuum).

In 1915, Einstein published a follow-up to his special relativity theory, general relativity, which generalises the above considerations to reference frames that are accelerating, particularly when the

---

[31] http://www.astronomy.ohio-state.edu/~pogge/Ast162/Unit5/gps.html

acceleration is that of gravity. This led to the famous curvature of space-time.

Indeed, General Relativity showed that heavy objects distort space-time, like a heavy ball curves a sheet of fabric. This too has some clear consequences, such as the deflection of star light when passing near a heavy object, e.g. the sun or a black hole, on its way to us. This was confirmed in 1919 when a solar eclipse presented the first opportunity for testing this prediction, and indeed telescopes showed light from distant stars bent by the sun's gravity, exactly as the theory had predicted. Similar effects have more recently been observed with black holes, which themselves are objects predicted by General Relativity, as they produce 'lensing' of light from stars or galaxies that lie 'behind' them (at large distances).

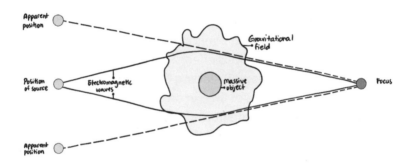

Figure 11 – *Bending of light when it passes near a massive object.*

Einstein's General Relativity was hugely important in another way: it could be applied to the universe as a whole. With a geometric conception and description of gravity, general relativity could apply to vast spaces and times, up to and including the entire universe. The fundamental equation in that theory was quickly solved by Einstein himself and afterwards by the Russian mathematician Alexander Friedman, and mathematical cosmology was thus born. The solutions implied a dynamic, evolving, and growing universe, something that Einstein rejected because it did not fit the 'paradigm' that his mind operated under. His philosophical worldview, that a universe without a beginning was much more symmetric and elegant and devoid of Judeo-Christian preconceptions, thus led him to modify his equation (by adding a 'cosmological constant' in a completely artificial manner) so as to produce a static solution. Ten years later, when the expansion of the universe was discovered (by Edwin Hubble, see below), Einstein called the modification he had made to his equation "his biggest blunder".

Einstein's theories of special and general relativity soon became two big pillars of modern physics. They completely changed our conception of the universe, from its origin to its evolution, and its large-scale structure and interactions (between stars and galaxies).

Quantum Mechanics is another pillar of modern physics that actually grew up alongside relativity in the early 20th century. If anything, Quantum Mechanics is even more bewildering and far-reaching than relativity—and much harder to explain. Two famous quotes about the theory, from physicists who contributed significantly to it, Niels Bohr and Richard Feynman, sum up the general view that even experts have of it: "If quantum mechanics hasn't profoundly shocked you, you haven't understood it" (Bohr), and, "I think I can safely say that nobody understands quantum mechanics" (Feynman).

Whereas the effects of relativity are felt mainly at very high speeds (some fraction of the speed of light) and large gravitational fields (close to stars and black holes), quantum mechanics applies at the lowest scales of size: atoms, nuclei and particles.

The first key idea in the theory relates to the word 'quantum', referring to the smallest amount of something, in this case energy, angular momentum, and other properties, which, the theory says, can only take discrete values, i.e. multiple amounts of the quantum (plural: quanta). Thus, energy cannot take any values on a continuous scale as it does in the classical (macroscopic, everyday) world; it is 'quantised'.

The second main idea of quantum physics is the wave-particle 'duality': all objects at the atomic level (from particles to molecules) can be regarded as waves as well as objects, depending on the circumstances, the same way it had been found that light sometimes behaves like waves and sometimes like a stream of particles ('photons').

The most famous consequence of this wave-particle duality is the 'uncertainty principle', which was formulated by Werner Heisenberg in 1927. This principle puts a limit on how much we can know about a quantum object: some quantities exclude each other from being measured simultaneously and very precisely. For instance, it is not possible to measure precisely an atom's position and speed at the same time.

And last but not least, quantum mechanics has been given an indeterministic and probabilistic interpretation.[32] Indeed, the Copenhagen group of pioneers of the theory (Bohr and his group) interpreted the theory as implying that while an object carries all possible states and values of its physical quantities, one can only give probabilities of getting this or that outcome when a measurement is performed. Nature is thus seen as 'indeterministic'; things can only be predicted with probabilities, and only statistical averages can be given for large systems.

Needless to say, this 'intrinsic indeterminacy' of the atomic and particle world has produced endless discussions and debates on what this means about the world, about God's creation, and many other big questions.

---

[32] This indeterministic and probabilistic interpretation is the dominant understanding of quantum mechanics among physicists, but there are minority views that present the theory in a deterministic approach. This is beyond the scope of this brief exposition.

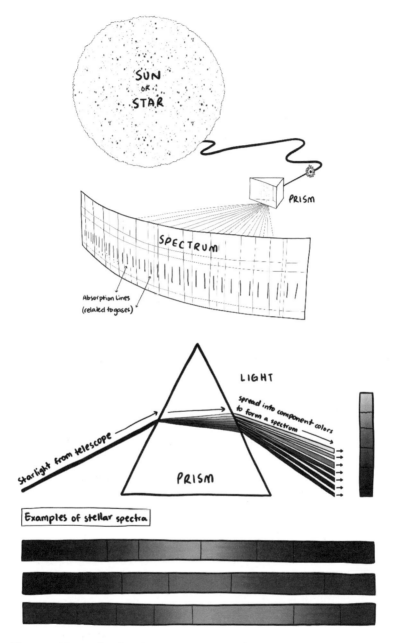

Figures 12a and 12b – *Spectroscopy: spreading and analysis of the light coming from the Sun (or other objects) to reveal various physical characteristics.*

Your Essential Astronomy and Cosmology

"Say: Contemplate what is in the heavens and the earth"

– Qur'an, 10:101

As we saw in our brief review of the history of science (Chapter 2), Modern Astronomy started with Copernicus replacing the earth with the sun at the centre of the 'world'. That fundamental shift was followed by Kepler's replacement of circles with ellipses for the orbits of the planets and Galileo reinventing the telescope and using it to observe the heavens and make groundbreaking discoveries. Within 50 years, Newton had produced a full mathematical and physical theory to explain why the planets (including Earth) revolve around the sun (its mass is much larger) and why orbits were elliptical. He also invented a new type of telescope (the reflector, based on mirrors) to replace the old refractor (based on lenses), due to the latter's defects (colour deformations, large lenses sagging under their weight, etc.). If that were not enough, Newton set physics on new, modern grounds, based on calculus and simple laws. Modern Astronomy had given birth to Modern Science.

Between the 17th and the early 20th century, astronomy, with larger telescopes and later the use of photographic plates to record images and analyse them carefully with plenty of time, discovered new planets (Uranus and Neptune) and started to take measure of the huge cosmic distances, particularly between stars. More importantly, in the second half of the 19th century, spectral analysis of the sun and other celestial objects (analysing the light received by spreading it through a prism to note the signatures of its gases), transformed astronomy into astrophysics.

It was in the early 20th century that new, big revolutions started to occur again in astronomy, or rather in cosmology, namely the study of the universe as a whole itself.

Cosmology – Big Bang

Cosmology became scientific and modern only after the publication of Einstein's theory of General Relativity in 1915, acquiring a firm mathematical foundation in Einstein's equations. Before that, cosmology was mostly speculative thinking, more or less guided by a mixture of astronomy, philosophy and oftentimes theology. It became scientific because it could make predictions, although observational tests were not immediately possible.

Soon cosmological observations and real data started to come in rich quantity and quality. In the 1920s Edwin Hubble (and a few less famous figures such as Henrietta Swan Leavitt and Vesto Slipher) performed truly revolutionary astronomical research. Hubble first proved that there are other galaxies besides the Milky Way, by establishing that the distance to the Andromeda galaxy (now known to be 2.5 million light-years from us) is far larger than the diameter of our Galaxy (now known to be 100,000 light-years). More astoundingly, a few years later he discovered that most galaxies are moving away from us, the so-called recession of galaxies. Hubble also established a relationship between the speed with which the galaxies were receding from us and the distances between us. Hubble's Law states that Velocity = H_0 × Distance, where H_0, known as the Hubble constant, which indicates the rate at which galaxies are collectively receding.

It is important to understand that this expansion of the universe is that of space-time itself: the galaxies are being dragged by the expanding space, which is curved, like little spots on the surface of a balloon that expands when blown into. In that analogy, the radius of the balloon represents time (zero at the centre, from which the balloon starts) and the surface representing the space which curves upon itself. From that one understands the idea of the 'observable universe'—the part that we can see from our position, since what is on 'the other side' we will never be able to see, with the universe continuing to expand.

People often ask: "But what is the universe expanding into?" The answer is: it is expanding in time, for what lies beyond the surface is future time, while space itself only expands. What makes the universe expand? The initial energy that burst from the initial point (of space time) is the answer to this question. Indeed, the entire universe, with space, time, and all its energy, started from a point. The whole universe was a point, thus there is no sense in asking 'where' that point was!

Georges Lemaitre was the first to realise that the expansion of the universe implies a start from something very small—what he called a 'primordial atom' of energy—or even from a point. Today we refer to that as the 'Big Bang', which can variously mean: a) the 'explosion' at the moment of creation; b) the first few moments (roughly minutes) of the universe, and what happened then; c) the entire theory of the physical evolution of the early universe.

If by 'Big Bang' one means the 'explosion' at the moment of creation, then we have no idea how that happened. Science may or may not be able to present a coherent and convincing explanation—or at least description—of that event (perhaps, some collision of previous universes or some other scenario), but for now, we have no solid model of what happened at t = 0.

If by 'Big Bang' one means the first few moments of the universe, then we know very well—and very precisely—what happened then and what the physical processes then produced. In brief, density and temperature started from infinitely high values, while the size of the universe was zero (or close to that). Expansion then led to a decrease in both the temperature and the density, and during the period 10^{-43} to 10^{-33}, a period of exponential 'inflation' took place, in which the universe expanded from the size of a proton to that of a grapefruit, which allowed for the energy to transform into particles: quarks, protons and neutrons. Once the temperature had dropped enough (to about 10 billion degrees Celsius), protons could fuse into helium nuclei, and the latter to some tiny amounts of lithium. This took about 3 minutes, after which the temperature had dropped too low for nuclear reactions to proceed. That is why 99% of the universe today is made up of hydrogen and helium (the two smallest nuclei/ elements); almost everything else (from carbon to uranium) was made much later in stars, where temperatures were high enough, in the core, to make heavy nuclei by way of nuclear fusion.

If by 'Big Bang' one means the entire theory of the physical evolution of the early universe, then today we do indeed have a very strong and coherent theory, well-supported by observational evidence.

What is the Evidence (the 'Proofs') for the Big Bang theory?

- The existence of a background radiation in all directions, with precisely the characteristics (mean energy and distribution in wavelengths) predicted by the Big Bang theory.

- The abundances of hydrogen (and its isotope deuterium), helium (plus its isotope He-3), and lithium, which we measure throughout the universe, are totally consistent (with an accuracy no less than 99.9%) with what the theory predicts.

- The very fact that the universe expands is consistent with the theory.

After the production of hydrogen, helium (and their isotopes), and lithium, the universe continued to expand until some 380,000 years later when the temperature had dropped below about 3,000 degrees. This temperature was sufficiently low that nuclei and electrons could bind and not be separated by collisions with enough thermal energy (heat) to separate them. When nuclei and electrons bind, they form atoms. The first atoms thus formed in the universe only about 380,000 years after the Big Bang.

The universe then continued to expand and cool, consequently large clouds of gas (almost entirely made of hydrogen and helium) formed here and there.

Since 1998, observational cosmologists have obtained solid data and convincing evidence that the universe has accelerated its expansion in the last few billion years. Yet how this happens is still unclear. Various ideas have been proposed under the general title of 'dark energy', a concept revisited at the end of this chapter. Current cosmological models stipulate that all matter and energy in the universe comprises 27% dark matter, 68% dark energy, and only 5% the normal matter that we are familiar with, from hydrogen to uranium.

Indeed, for decades now, astronomers and physicists have become almost unanimously convinced of the existence of a form of matter dubbed 'dark' due to its lack of electromagnetic interaction. This is because while it exchanges no light or radiation with any other particle, it exerts a significant gravitational effect, especially at the large scales of galaxies, clusters of galaxies, and the universe as a whole. The search for particles of this type has so far been unsuccessful, but this ingredient is essential in the general cosmological picture.

If 95% of the universe's content is not yet known or understood, clearly cosmology still has much work to do, and predictions of the universe's future are at present largely speculative: one can easily construct models that are consistent with all current knowledge and which predict an eternal expansion, a 'big crunch', or even a 'big rip'.

Finally, cosmologists have been puzzled by two striking features of the universe. First, amounts of normal matter, dark matter, dark energy, and radiation are currently all within a factor of 5 to 10 of each other—this is referred to as 'the coincidence problem'. Second, many of the universe's parameters and physical laws *had* to be almost exactly what they are in our universe for any complex structures—and life and humans—to form. This is known as the 'fine-tuning' issue. Proposals to explain this invoke either the 'anthropic principle', a meta-scientific principle which the universe satisfies, or the multiverse, assuming the existence of zillions of universes, each with its different physical construction, with only one or a few having the appropriate features to produce complexity, life, and humans. Direct observation of other universes is not possible, but perhaps indirect evidence can be produced. Here, one begins to touch the limits of modern cosmology.

One question that people often ask is: "Can we talk about 'before the Big Bang'?" Yes and no. No, if we agree that time starts with the big bang; it is then like asking about "north of the North Pole"— it makes no sense. But yes, if (as some cosmologists have recently been proposing), our universe could have emerged from the collision of other universes.

Galaxies, Stars, and Planets

Other remarkable leaps in astronomical knowledge include:

a) The realisation that the observable universe contains 100+ billion galaxies of different kinds, some of them are 'active' (with a massive black hole at the centre swallowing matter and producing huge amounts of energy and radiation in the process).

b) The discovery of a variety of stars, from dead and compact ones (black holes, neutron stars, and white dwarfs) to supergiants (billions of times bigger than our sun, which is an average one).

c) The discovery (in the last 20 years) of a zoo of previously unimagined 'exoplanets' (planets outside our solar system, i.e. revolving around stars in the galaxy, some relatively close to us and some rather far), with various 'strange' cases (planets revolving around 2, 3, 4 stars) and countless ones residing in the 'habitable zone', where the temperature is between 0 and 100 Celsius, thus raising the possibility of the existence of life, at least of the primitive kind.

Another important progress in our understanding of the cosmos was the development of a solid theory of the formation and evolution of the solar system, starting from a big cloud/nebula 4.5 billion years ago. This is important because: a) it implies a 'deep time' or 'big history' for humans, life, planets, and the cosmos; b) it directly conflicts with the beliefs that some religious communities hold, namely that creation (of earth and everything else) took place less than 10,000 years ago. This is not a problem that we find among Muslim groups, but it points to the need to read and interpret scriptures non-literally on many such topics.

An Amazing Universe		
Galaxies	**Stars**	**Exoplanets**

Succinctly, a big cloud of gas (a few light-years across), made mostly of hydrogen and helium with less than 1% of the heavier elements (carbon, oxygen, nitrogen, iron etc.) was pulled inward by gravity, resulting in the formation of a star (our sun) with 99% of the initial mass. Solid pieces in regions farther away from the Sun coalesced gradually to form 'planetesimals' (miniature planets), then 'proto-planets' i.e. planets that have not yet completed their formation processes, are still cooling and solidifying etc. These will make 'rocky' planets like Earth, the 'terrestrial planets'.

FORMATION OF SOLAR SYSTEM FROM NEBULA

1. NEBULA INITIALLY

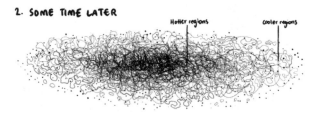

2. SOME TIME LATER

3. FEW MILLION YEARS LATER

4. SOME TIME LATER

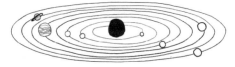

5. 100 MILLION YEARS LATER

Figure 13 – *Formation of the Sun and the planets from the original solar nebula (cloud).*

In regions farther still from the Sun, where the temperature is much lower, planets formed and were able to retain large amounts of gases, making 'Jovian planets' (Jupiter-like). Between the two groups of planets and rocky pieces that couldn't come together, for lack of sufficient gravitational 'glue' to form a planet, they jointly/collectively became a 'belt' of asteroids. On the outskirts of the solar system, mountain-size chunks of matter mixed solid elements with icy water, making comets. All of these remained under the gravitational 'control' of the sun, revolving around it. Hence, all of these (sun, planets, asteroids and comets) make up the solar system: everything revolving around the sun, under the effect of its gravitational pull.

Earth then gradually cooled and underwent geological activity, with volcanoes in particular spewing out carbon dioxide, methane and other gases. With comets and asteroids that carry water bombarding the planet very frequently in the early periods of the solar system's history, and Earth residing in the 'habitable zone', where the temperature is moderate and water can be liquid, oceans and seas and lakes appeared. At some point, life of the most primitive kind (bacteria and algae) appeared in the waters. Then photosynthesis led to the absorption of the carbon dioxide in the atmosphere and the release of oxygen, which further helped develop life (aerobic organisms)…

Your Essential Biology

In 2013, researchers at Brigham Young University (USA) conducted a survey[33] among professors, biology and science students, and non-science students, asking them "what biological concepts are, in their opinion, most important for their education." The professors and the students were asked to rank the following 17 topics from most to least important: the Cell; Cell Division; Biological Molecules; the Central Dogma; Evolution; Mendelian Genetics; Ecology; Bioen-

---

[33] Howell, J. R. et al. (2013), What Biology Concepts are Important in General Education?: A Survey of Faculty Members and Students, *Science Education and Civic Engagement*, 5:1, pp. 38-45.

ergetics (cellular respiration); Photosynthesis; Metabolism and Enzymes; Plant Reproduction; Embryonic Development; Immunology; Viruses; Fundamentals of Chemistry; History of Science and Scientific Reasoning/Method.

Interestingly, the three groups; professors, biology and science students, and non-science students, differed significantly in what they regarded as most and least important topics and concepts.

For professors, the three concepts most frequently ranked as important were: Scientific Reasoning, the Cell, and Evolution. The bottom three were: Viruses, Immunology, and Embryonic Development.

Both science and non-science students had the same top three topics: the Cell, Biological Molecules, and Cell Division. Amazingly, Evolution was near the bottom for both student groups: 13th and 14th, respectively, out of 17. Moreover, Ecology was ranked 8th by the professors, 15th by non-science majors and 17th (dead bottom) by biology and science students! Interestingly, 'Scientific Reasoning' was ranked 4th by biology and science students and 8th by non-science students. And last but not least, 'History of Science' was ranked 12th by the professors, 16th by the science students, and 17th (last) by the non-science students.

There is clearly some significant disconnect between what Biology professors consider to be very important topics to teach and what students, particularly the non-science majors, perceive as important. The authors of the study thus conclude: "Given this scenario, perhaps our best and most creative teachers should be given the assignment of teaching our non-major students." This chapter and this whole book is in line with that recommendation…

Cells

Cells constitute the basic building blocks of life, as all living organisms are made of (many) cells, though the most basic organisms, bacteria, are made of only one cell.

Cells were discovered in 1665 by Robert Hooke, the British scientist and contemporary of Newton. This was the result of looking at living matter (plants and animals) through a microscope (which was invented around the year 1620, shortly after the telescope, in 1608). 'Cells', i.e. little compartments, were seen to resemble little rooms in big buildings such as castles or prisons. More than a century later (in the 1800s), two German scientists uncovered the connection between life and cells: Matthias Schleiden for plants, and Theodor Schwann for animals, the two categories of living organisms being shown to be fundamentally different.

Schleiden's and Schwann's discoveries thus gave birth to 'modern biology' with their starting of 'cell theory', which includes a set of *rules* for how living organisms function.

First and foremost, all cells come from previous cells, in a process known as cellular division.

Secondly, cells are divided into two types: a) the simpler 'prokaryotic' ones are without a nucleus, they make prokaryotes (prokaryotic organisms), which are usually unicellular; b) those with a nucleus, known as eukaryotic cells, make eukaryotes, which normally consist of many cells working together. Both types of cells have membranes (envelopes), but eukaryotes also have organelles, which are sub-units inside the cell with their own membranes, and play a specific role, such as producing food for the cell. The largest organelle in a eukaryote is the nucleus, which acts as a control centre for the cell.

In plants and animals, cells form tissues of various organs that make up a 'system' (nervous, digestive, respiratory system etc.), which together constitute a fully functioning body. Bodies are

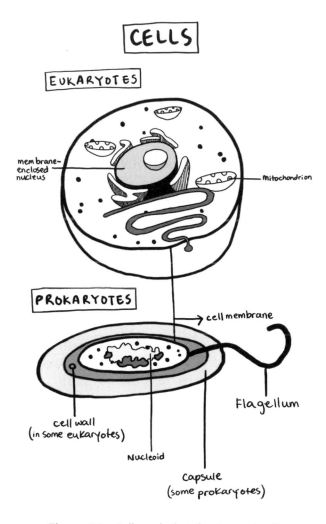

Figure 14 – *Cells and what they're made of.*

usually part of a large group, i.e. a population, a community or an ecosystem.

Plants and animals can be simply characterised as food producers and consumers. Plants use energy from light to make sugar from carbon dioxide and water, releasing oxygen as a by-product (through the photosynthesis process). Plants combine these sugars with minerals from the soils to make carbohydrates, proteins and fats, which are stored in the plant's cells.

Animals get their food by eating plants and other animals. They break down those big molecules by a general process called metabolism, which uses a variety of chemical processes. The essential molecules thus obtained, as well as the energy thus released, allow the cells in the body to carry out their functions.

Cell operations are based on molecular interactions that keep things working properly and steadily. Living systems are made of complex molecules that consist mostly of a few elements, mainly carbon, hydrogen, oxygen, nitrogen, and phosphorous. Cell operations ensure the following essential things: a) that energy is absorbed from the environment (in the form of food or light) and processed (e.g. food is burned with oxygen to release heat which is then transferred to various parts of the body for various needs); b) that the cell, organ, system and body are protected (from outside effects); c) that the cell and the body can reproduce to survive.

But how do cells and organs know what to do, what to transfer where, what to store and what to consume, etc.? Part of the answer is in the laws (of physics and chemistry) that underlie those interactions: by their structures and energy levels, molecules will interact one way or another, consume or release energy, and that automatically works in the way a cell should. A larger part of the answer, regarding the more complex operations of a cell or organ or body, resides in the codes of information and processes that cells carry in their DNA, or more specifically in their genes.

Different species are characterised by different genomes—the entire set of genes that make up the DNA, which makes up the chromosomes that are found in the nucleus of every cell (see Figure 15). Each cell, therefore, carries the complete information about any given individual. During reproduction, the cell divides into two identical cells, and each carries the same full information—except when an error happens during the replication or a mutation occurs due to some external effect e.g. radiation hitting the DNA molecule at some point.

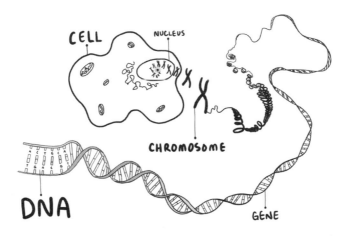

Figure 15 – *The cell's nucleus, the chromosomes, the genes, and the DNA.*

In sexual reproduction, the male and the female contribute one set of chromosomes, and the newborn individual is then a 'mixture' of the parents; for humans, the 23 pairs of chromosomes are split, and the baby gets 23 from each of his/her parents. Sometimes, however, slight changes occur, due to the errors or mutations I just mentioned. Over time, these slight differences, if they are not lethal, accumulate and make the descendants differ from their ancestors, to the point sometimes of deviating so much from the original species (for example wings may gradually appear) to make them a new, different species. This process is called biological evolution.

Genetics

Genes, segments of the DNA, number in the thousands, and make up a chromosome (see Figure 15). More importantly, they carry the 'coded' and essential information that tells each cell and each organ how to behave (chemically), most notably how to make specific protein molecules. The genes are passed on to the offspring by the rules of heredity.

Any changes to a DNA segment, changes which can occur naturally (mutations or errors) or artificially (genetic 'engineering'), by deleting, inserting, or substituting a molecular piece at the appropriate place, can alter a specific gene. Genes, or portions of them, can be taken from other animals or plants or can even be artificially constructed. This can be harmful or advantageous to the organism, or in some cases it can make no noticeable difference.

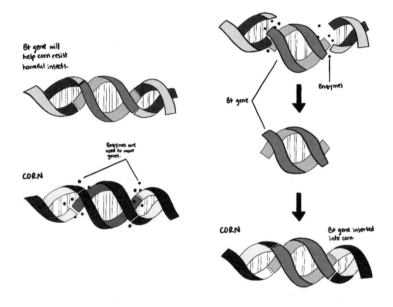

Figure 16 – *Genetic manipulations/engineering.*

Needless to say, the religious and ethical issues raised by genetic manipulations are diverse and complex. We will address them in the next chapter.

Evolution

The idea of biological evolution, i.e. that animals and plants change over a short or long time in different environments, was noted from antiquity. It was 'understood' that the environment 'pushes' plants and animals to 'adapt' to changing conditions. Such ideas could be found in the writings of thinkers and scholars from Aristotle (384–322 BCE) in Greece to Al-Jahiz (776–868 CE) in the Arab-Islamic civilisation and up to Lamarck (1744–1829) in France.

It was Charles Darwin (1809–1882), however, who realised that the environment is only responsible for the changes that occur in living organisms through mutations, though he didn't use this word and didn't understand how such sudden changes in the internal constituents of the organism occurred. Darwin understood that such changes can be positive or negative, useful or destructive to the organism, and it is the environment that selects the good changes as they give a survival advantage to those that have had such changes compared to those that have not had them or have had negative ones.

The simplest example is the giraffe: giraffes may be born whose necks are longer, shorter, stronger, or weaker, due to mutations or replication errors at the cellular level, but since a longer neck allows giraffes to feed on taller trees, the short-neck giraffes will soon die and only the long-neck giraffes will reproduce and multiply. After some time, all giraffes will have long necks and will differ significantly from their ancestors. The same thing happened with small dinosaurs: when mutations produced some skin in their arms and forearms, this was selected by the environment when it became cold. That skin then evolved into feathers, even more efficient at keeping warm. Soon those feathers were large enough to allow the small dinosaurs to make flying jumps, thus escaping predators such as bigger dinosaurs. Further evolution allowed those 'dinosaurs' to fly, thus becoming birds. New and completely different species thus evolved in this way.

Evidence for this general evolutionary scenario can be found in countless fossils of various animals, which when dated using radioactive isotopes, allow us to reconstitute the entire history of those species. But today we have stronger evidence: the genetic record of various species, which we can extract from cells and compare, again tracing the changes over time and seeing which species relates most to which and at what point it broke from an earlier common 'parent'.

Evolution is therefore the result of two main effects: mutations and errors that modify one particular gene or another, and natural selection by the environment—which includes the limited supply of available resources required for life as well as the potential of a population to increase its numbers.

The Evidence ('Proofs') for Evolution

The Fossil Record: 'Missing Links' are No Longer Missing!

The radioactive dating of fossils allows us to reconstruct their history and 'genealogy', invariably confirming the predictions of evolution for various species and the transitions that have generated new species.

Many transitional species have been found during the last few decades: from fish to reptiles, reptiles to birds and great apes to humans. "Thousands of intermediate fossil remains [including for humans] have been discovered since Darwin's time, and the rate of discovery is accelerating."[34]

Genetic Evidence

With the recent decoding of the genomes of many species, including humans, chimpanzees, and gorillas, it has been shown[35] that humans have approximately 96% of common DNA with chimpanzees, a little less with the gorillas, much less with rhesus monkeys and so

---

[34] Ibid, p. 9.

[35] The Chimpanzee Sequencing and Analysis Consortium, "Initial sequence of the chimpanzee genome and comparison with the human genome", Nature, Sept. 1, 2005, no. 437, p. 69-87. See also Charlesworth & Charlesworth, op. cit., p. 103, and Ayala , op. cit., p. 108.

on. More striking and specific evidence can be found:[36] We humans have 46 chromosomes, while monkeys have 48, but our chromosome #2 turns out to be exactly the chimpanzees' chromosomes #12 and #13 tied together in a strange and totally unique way; at some point in the evolution of primates, those two chromosomes merged into one in humans but not other apes...

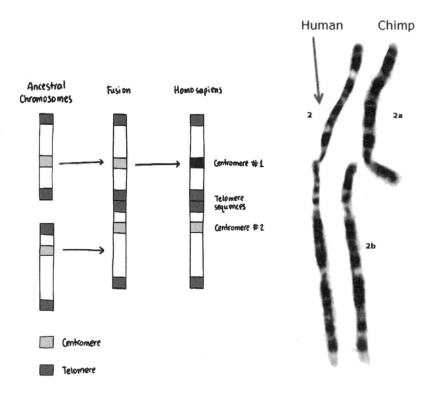

Figure 17 - *Illustration[37] of the fusion of chromosomes 12 and 13 of chimpanzee, making the human chromosome #2.*

[36] Kenneth R. Miller, *"Only a Theory. Evolution and the battle for America's soul"*, Penguin Books, 2008.
[37] Ibid.

Comparative Anatomy

Comparisons between parts of bodies of animals that may seem totally unrelated to each other (e.g. a monkey, a horse, a dolphin and a bat) lead to the conclusion that they must have emerged from a common ancestor. For example, the comparison of the bone structure of their limbs (feet, hands, arms, wings) easily shows that they are all equipped with five 'fingers', despite the very different ways they use them: the monkey grasps with the hand, the horse gallops on its hooves, the dolphin swims with its fins, and the bat flies with its wings. This can be explained by the fact that these limbs are the result of an evolution from a common amphibian ancestor.

Universal Biochemical Organisation

The fact that the biochemical organisation of all organisations are based on the same genetic coding in DNA, is further evidence of the commonality of species in nature. In fact, a DNA fragment will represent the same amino acid in a bacterium, a human cell, a plant or an animal. Indeed, the Nobel Prize for Medicine was awarded in 2001 to scientists who had shown that the gene involved in the control system of yeast cells is the same one that mutates in some human cancers.

Human Evolution

Humans have long been noticed to greatly resemble gorillas and other apes. For example, the name 'orangutan' comes from the aborigines' *orang*, meaning 'man' and *utan*, forest. This similarity between man and apes, in both their physiologies and their lifestyles, was also noted and described at length by several classical-era Muslim authors.[38] Furthermore, as I have mentioned, modern genetics has established not only extensive similarities but also points of

---

[38] Mahfuz Ali Azzam, *"Mabda' at-Tatawwur al-Hayawiyy lada Falasifat al-Islam"* ("The Principle of Biological Evolution in the Works of the Classical Muslim Philosophers"), Al-Mu'assassah al-Jami`iyyah li-d-Dirassat wa-l-Nashr wa-t-Tawzi', Beirut, Lebanon, 1996, pp. 117-118.

'contact' in the genomes of humans and various apes. This similarity is strong evidence that we have a common ancestor, and the genetic 'points of contact' allow us to determine a 'point of separation' at around 5.4 to 6.3 million years ago.[39] However, as Ayala insists: "in some *biological* respects we are very similar to apes, but in other biological respects we are very different, and these differences provide a valid foundation for a religious view of humans as special creatures of God"[40] (emphasis by Ayala).

Do we have fossils that we can consider as evidence of such transitions (from apes to humans), the famous 'missing links'? Yes, indeed, and the evidence keeps mounting, and fast. Briefly, one can refer to Lucy, the hominid dating back to 3.2 million years ago that was found in Ethiopia in 1974 and which has 'mixed' human-ape characteristics: only 1.10m tall, weighing 29kg, with a small brain (only about a third of modern humans'), and with long arms, all similar to chimpanzees, but walking upright in human locomotion. One may also mention 'Lucy's baby', a 3.3 million year old skeleton that was found uncovered in Ethiopia in 2006 and which was described as "a very good transitional species... a mixture of ape-like and human-like features."[41]

In the past few years, dozens of such skeletons (usually partial) have been uncovered. One of them, for example, known as *Australopithecus garhi*, dates back to 2.5 million years and is considered as a prime candidate for the link that paleontologists have been searching for between Lucy and us. Most importantly, its discoverers have advanced circumstantial evidence that *A. garhi* was able to make tools. This would represent the real start of humans taking off from their animal ancestry.

But as I briefly mention in the sidebar, the genetic evidence for evolution in general, and human evolution in particular, is now the strongest line of evidence. Perhaps the most striking example is

---

[39] *Science et Vie* Hors Series, no. 235, June 2006, p. 18, referring to a paper in *Nature* but without full citation.

[40] Ayala, op. cit., pp. 105-106.

[41] http://news.bbc.co.uk/2/hi/science/nature/5363328.stm

that of the merging of chromosomes 12 and 13 of the chimpanzees into chromosome #2 in humans (see Figure 17). But there are also other good examples. For instance, humans need vitamin C to help produce collagen, an important protein that prevents scurvy (a degeneration of the gums that can lead to death). Other mammals can produce vitamin C in their own bodies, but we cannot, because we lack an essential enzyme, gulonolactone oxidase (GLO), due to a bad mutation which occurred at some point in the past. The genomes show that close primates, such as chimpanzees and gorillas, also do not have this enzyme (but get vitamin C from fruits they consume each day), while more distant primates do not have this deficiency; the mutation occurred during the evolution of these species, and we can locate it in time (millions of years ago).

Another quick example (among many others) is the haemoglobin protein (which makes blood red), is composed of two genes, one of which ('a pseudo-gene') is in our chromosome #16; gorillas and chimpanzees have exactly the same configuration in their genomes.

More generally, the sequencing of the human genome, as well as that of many other animals, has shown that not only is the number of genes we have remarkably small (about 21,000 genes)[42] of 3 billion nucleobases (represented by the letters A, C, G, T in the DNA), but it is the same for most other animals whose genes are, again, very often almost exactly the same as ours. Between humans and chimpanzees, the difference between the bases of DNA is about 1.2%; other ways to compare the genomes of the two species give more than 4% of difference.[43]

To sum up, I want to strongly emphasise the wealth of evidence we now have for evolution, both biological (across all organisms) and human evolution, particularly since the advent of genetics (although fossils have now been found in such great numbers and diversity that they too have become a very strong line of evidence,

---

[42] https://www.genome.gov/DNADay/q.cfm?aid=2&year=2012

[43] The Chimpanzee Sequencing and Analysis Consortium, 'Initial sequence of the chimpanzee genome and comparison with the human genome', *Nature* 437, 69-87 (1 September 2005).

---

and the old 'missing links' are no longer missing). No educated person can deny that evolution is a fact of nature's history. What is not completely settled, however, is the theory that explains in all details how various aspects of evolution occurred. Most experts agree that the neo-Darwinian theory constitutes a very good framework and can explain much of the evidence, but a small but respectable minority insists that some aspects of the theory are in need of revamping. This is normal; as I have explained, theories are improved or even transformed all the time in all fields of science. One must not think that because the theory of evolution is not 100% finalised that the facts of evolution can be ignored or denied.

What Remains to be Known?

What Next in Physics?

The biggest challenge facing theoretical physics today is how to combine general relativity (Einstein's theory of gravity, which defeats Newton's for strong gravity cases) with quantum mechanics (which applies only at the smallest scales). Combining the two is needed for the very shortest times in the Big Bang, i.e. 10^{-43} seconds, when the universe was 10^{-35} m big (100 billion billion times smaller than an atomic nucleus) and gravity was humongous (with all the matter and energy concentrated in that small space).

Physicists have successfully combined electricity with magnetism (Maxwell), then electromagnetism with the weak nuclear force (Abdus Salam, Weinberg, and Glashow, who received the 1979 Nobel Prize for their work), then with the strong nuclear force (the standard model of particle physics), but gravity has resisted any unification with the rest. Some serious 'theories' have been proposed, most notably String Theory, but none have had any experimental confirmation or even any consensus among theorists.

The quantum revolution has now moved on to technological applications, in electronics, with the continuing efforts to miniaturise chips, but more promisingly and fascinatingly in nanotechnology, with the possibility of building atom-size robots that can perform a wide array of tasks in different domains. From biotechnology and medicine to energy, industry, and environmental applications, and in 'quantum computing', which makes use of quantum effects (superposition, entanglement) to greatly multiply the ability to store and transfer information beyond the simple binary (0 and 1) system of normal computers. Furthermore, 'teleportation' of objects (transferring all their information and characteristics from one place to another one in no time), once the subject of science fiction, has now become a reality—at least for particles, with the dream of enlarging the scope of 'teleportation' to bigger and bigger molecules, and perhaps in the future to cells and living organisms…

And lastly, also in the realm of applications of science, efforts to achieve a fusion nuclear reactor that produces more energy than it consumes are still under way. The International Thermonuclear Experimental Reactor (ITER) currently in construction in France is supposed to start operations in 2020 and run full fusion reactions in 2027. Whether it will achieve large-scale fusion with positive energy balance, and whether the cost of the project will point to a future of cheap energy or not remains to be seen.

What Next in Astronomy and Cosmology?

In Astronomy, the current hottest field is the ongoing search for exoplanets, particularly earth-sized ones in habitable zones, with the ultimate prize of finding life, whether primitive or evolved, anywhere in the Milky Way. Searches in other galaxies are technically unfeasible, due to the large distances and the extremely weak light signals we receive from any individual star in those galaxies, let alone from planets orbiting around them.

New giant telescopes that will see the light in a few years will attempt to detect 'bio-signatures' in the light they will record from the promising (earth-sized) exoplanets in our galaxy, by finding 'fingerprints' of life in the spectra from those planets, i.e. the presence of gases such as oxygen, ozone, or methane, that give strong indications of the existence of life there.

Optimistic astronomers believe that this major goal will be achieved within 10 years or so; others think it may take a few decades...

The existence of life elsewhere, whether primitive or advanced, perhaps even more advanced than us[44] clearly raises philosophical and religious questions of "what is our place and importance in the universe?" Whether we are alone in this galaxy/universe or we are one of billions of species, from bacteria to super-intelligent ones, calls for reflection. We will explore that question in the next chapter.

In Cosmology, there are two very big questions awaiting definitive answers from researchers: a) what is 'dark energy', which is theorised to be responsible for the acceleration of the expansion of the universe, which was discovered in 1998 and confirmed in a number of satellite measurements of cosmic objects; b) what is 'dark matter', the type of massive objects that populate the cosmos (about five times more than the mass-energy of all light-emitting matter in the universe) and which acts only gravitationally, not electromagnetically.

The effects of 'dark energy' can be seen on the expansion of the universe, or more specifically on the recession of faraway galaxies, and there have been a number of theoretical propositions about what that kind of energy it could come from, but so far we have not gathered enough observational evidence to pinpoint the nature of that 'dark energy'. Indeed, some cosmologists have suggested that the acceleration of the expansion of the universe might even be due to other effects, e.g. the need for a modification of Einstein's General Relativity, though this is largely rejected by the community.

---

[44] Recall that life on Earth has only existed for the last 3-4 billion years, yet the Milky Way has existed for about 12 billion years, thus life elsewhere would have had a long time to appear and thus evolve beyond what has been achieved on earth...

The effects of dark matter can be seen on the dynamics of stars within galaxies as well as that of galaxies within clusters of galaxies, and it has been the subject of experimental searches for some time, but still no solid detection has been reported. This could change quickly, should any laboratory or accelerator report the discovery of such a particle, and that would be a huge breakthrough, as big as the discovery of the Higgs particle if not bigger.

What Next in Biology?

The biggest question in Biology today is how life started. Some scientists believe this problem will be solved within a decade or two, others think it may never be figured out—that it is too complex! Many people think that it is a taboo question: dealing with 'God's creation prerogative'. They say that going from inert matter to living organisms is an act of creation, an act that only God performs, hence science shouldn't even try to figure it out… Needless to say, this is a wrongheaded approach. Just like astronomy figured out how earth was 'created', with its beautiful waters and atmosphere and geology, allowing life to appear and prosper, likewise science can (in principle) figure out how complex molecules at some point acquired the capacity to replicate and to preserve themselves, the two characteristics of life. We have already explained (briefly) how life then evolves, in a very natural way.

We shall come back to this question of the origin of life in the next chapter, when we discuss Islamic positions with regard to all the scientific issues we have raised.

Another area of active research is to finalise or fine-tune the theory of evolution, which currently is dominated by the Darwinian approach, but we have recently seen calls for perhaps some additions to the main theoretical framework of evolution. Darwinian ideas, i.e. mutations and natural selection, will certainly remain the basis, but perhaps some additional effects might be needed as well. In particular, the idea of 'convergence', that some features of living organisms (eyes, body symmetry, etc.) are arrived at by many different evolutionary routes and therefore seem 'inscribed' in nature. Some scientists insist that this idea adds something important to the overall view of life's evolution.

More importantly for the general public, particularly the religious public, is the issue of human evolution, with new discoveries, such as new skeletons and new genetic analyses, being regularly reported. We do have a general timeline for the evolution of humans, but some parts of it are still in need of solid confirmation, from the most recent past (how much interaction did our ancestors have with the Neanderthals, when did these disappear, what about the other species of 'humans', e.g. *Homo floresiensis* and *Homo georgicus*) to the most distant one, several million years ago when splits occurred in the ape tree (Australopithecus to gorillas, chimpanzees, and humans)… There are a number of minor points and details to be figured on the science front. And needless to say, there is much work to be done to harmonise this scenario with the religious conception of humans and their history. We shall also come back to this in the next chapter.

On the genetic front, important progress is being made in identifying various genes responsible (at least in part) for this or that disease or for this or that human physical or mental characteristic. This has important consequences in biology and medicine, with the era of 'personalised' medicine already under way. Not only that, but the field of genetic engineering/modification and even of 'synthetic biology' (with CRISPR, the recent popular technique of gene editing, opening the door for any small lab to play genetic manipulator) has simultaneously raised hopes for revolutionary fixing of flaws that each of us carries but also concerns of a dangerous tomorrow. One bad move and a dangerous bacteria or virus can be created, or perhaps monsters (in their bodies or their minds), or humans with all the super-capabilities that money can buy…

The Adventure Continues

Even with all these exciting future prospects, one must remain humble and expect the unexpected. Indeed, the simple and true answer to the question "what remains to be known?" is: everything else. The history of science, especially in the last few centuries of modern science, has shown us that the universe is more incredible than we can imagine or possibly comprehend, and each new discovery opens new doors and windows onto vast areas of untapped unknown.

Shakespeare had eloquently summed this thought in Hamlet:

> "There are more things in heaven and earth, Horatio,
> Than are dreamt of in your philosophy."

And Karl Popper, the premier 20th century philosopher of science, also expressed that idea nicely: "Our knowledge can only be finite, while our ignorance must necessarily be infinite."

The scientific adventure of discovery continues, greater than ever...

CHAPTER 5
·················
What Does Islam Say about Those Science Topics?

"Say: Contemplate what is in the heavens and the earth."
(Qur'an, 10:101)

How to Mesh Modern Science with the Qur'an

WE HAVE COME A LONG way from the old science of the Greeks, the Indians, the Chinese, and even that of the golden age Arab-Muslim civilisation... Earth is no longer the centre of the cosmos; the universe is staggeringly larger and more varied than anyone had dreamed; nature is infinitely more complex and fascinating than even the greatest minds of the past had imagined; life and humanity have undergone vast evolution, recorded in the rocks of earth and in the DNA of our cells... Most importantly, do these huge developments and new views on the universe and the human species conflict with our religious (Islamic) teachings? What does all this say about God as a Creator and Sustainer of the world(s) and His (special) relation to us? Are all those scientific theories acceptable to Islam/Muslims?

The first and most essential thing that we must clarify and stress is that facts cannot be denied on any basis; this would be like stating the sun is not up when everyone else can see it in the sky! Whatever has been confirmed by objective methods (by different people and groups, in different settings, by various procedures, etc.) must be accepted.

Most people will say "that's fine", at least in principle, although many will not always know how to distinguish 'facts' from 'hypotheses', 'models' from 'theories', etc. This is where the explanations and examples that I gave in Chapter 3 are so important.

Muslims (and others) usually don't raise objections to 'facts', unless they clearly imply something they do not (at least initially) want to accept (such as evolution); the doubts are most often expressed with regard to 'theories', the usual: "But evolution is a theory, not a fact, so why do I have to accept it?"

This is where we need to differentiate between full-fledged scientific theories (Big Bang, Evolution, Relativity, Quantum Mechanics etc.) and between hypotheses and conjectures. The best example to give here is the multiverse. A large number of physicists have postulated the existence of billions of universes beyond ours, universes that differ from ours in their characteristics (different laws, different types of particles, different values for parameters such as the speed of light, the expansion rate etc.), like bubbles appearing in the soapy foam, some remaining stable and others falling back into the foam at various points in time (a mega-time, before and after our own universe). The reason for postulating these hypotheses is twofold: a) one doesn't then need to explain the origin of our own universe or answer the question "what was there before the Big Bang?"; and b) this provides an 'explanation' to the fine-tuned parameters of our universe, the fact that if the values of the speed of light, the charge of the electron, the mass of the proton, the strength of gravity, the rate of expansion, and many others, had been different by even a small amount, not only would we not be here, life could not have appeared, and no complex structures (galaxies, stars, planets, etc.) could have formed. If there are zillions of universes out there with different parameters, then surely one of them at least would (by chance) have the right characteristics. This still would not explain where this entire multiverse comes from, but that's another problem. The point here is that this is a conjecture, a hypothesis; it has been given some elaborate theoretical underpinning ('eternal inflation', 'landscape', etc.), but it has no experimental or observational support of any kind. Indeed, most physicists doubt that we will ever be able to confirm this as a bona fide theory, at the same level of confirmation and solidity as Einstein's theories, Newton's laws, Darwin's theory etc.

So it all comes down to the important scientific methodology that I explained and stressed in Chapter 3: once we can clearly put an idea into one of those categories (hypotheses, facts, laws, models, theories), then we can determine the level of certainty we have about them, and then we can conclude whether we must accept them or not. In a nutshell: facts *must* be accepted; laws are useful but might be modified in the future to be made closer to what they describe (Newton's law of gravity subsided by Einstein's equation of gravity/general relativity); hypotheses and models are ideas and working tools for scientists; theories are largely true, but they can and often are modified and improved upon by incorporating additional features. For example, Darwin's theory was gradually modified by adding genetic mutations, then sexual selection and other features, some minor and some major. But the general framework remains the same, so one can still speak of 'Darwin's theory of evolution.'

That is how we determine what we must accept, what we can suspend judgement on, and of course what we can and must reject: gratuitous claims that not only have no experimental or observational support but run against the general accepted scientific knowledge.

Now, many Muslims often ask: but what about Qur'anic verses that 'clearly' conflict with some of those scientific facts or theories? Most Muslims add: "For me, the Qur'an is above any science, it overrules science if the latter makes any claim that conflict with some of its verses".

Here we must clarify two essential principles: 1) the Qur'an is not a book of science; it is a book of guidance; any examples it gives about nature are not supposed to be descriptive but rather enlightening, pointing to some meaningful idea; 2) interpreting Qur'anic verses is often a subjective exercise, which is why we have many ex-egeses that not only interpret some verses in different ways (some-times complementary, sometimes very different) but often fall into very different schools of thought (Sunni, Shi'i, Mu`tazili, Sufi, etc.) or categories (linguistic, socio-historic, modern, juristic, objectivist, etc.). Indeed, except when verses are referring to basic principles of Islam, in which cases all exegetical efforts will pretty much say the same thing, hundreds of verses will be interpreted differently by different commentators depending on their philosophical inclina-tions or understanding of the message of the Qur'an.

From this we conclude two important things: 1) the Qur'an, be-ing a book of guidance, is entirely concerned with issues of pur-pose and of human life, which relates and exists within nature and the universe; that is how the many Qur'anic verses on nature and the cosmos must be viewed and understood. Then, 2) Science and the Qur'an have very different methodologies: science is inductive, it starts from what we see in nature and builds laws and theories to explain the observed phenomena, and it aims to be objective, independent of who makes the observations, the experiments, or the theoretical frameworking; the Qur'an, while presenting a logi-cal discourse with arguments and examples that the mind can fol-low and be convinced of, is mainly concerned with building *faith* and a relationship between humans and God, humans with each other, and between humans and the world (environment, cosmos). The two approaches and goals are complementary, but they can-not trespass on each other's turf, and they certainly cannot over-rule one another.

So just like we believers do not allow atheists and materialists to use their science to claim that religious concepts are false (no God, no spirit etc.), we cannot allow religious views to veto out any sci-entific results, at least if they fall in the 'facts' or 'theories' categories.

So how do we mesh science and Islam without committing the methodological errors I have just mentioned? The great Muslim philosopher, jurist, physician, and astronomer Ibn Rushd (1126–

1198) presented a simple approach to how faith and reason can be harmonised (see his beautiful short book *Fasl al-Maqal* ('The Definitive Discourse').[45] He writes: "Truth (Revelation) cannot contradict wisdom (philosophy i.e. rational, demonstrative methods); on the contrary, they must agree with each other and support (stand with) each other."

Then what does one do when confronted with a situation where in all appearances the Revealed Text conflicts with the conclusions reached by Reason/Philosophy/Science? Ibn Rushd says clearly: whenever there is such an apparent contradiction, the (religious) Text must be allegorically understood and subjected to interpretation by those whom the Qur'an calls 'rooted in knowledge' (Q 3:7), who in Ibn Rushd's view are those who wield the highest methods of knowledge. He further insists that the Qur'an lends itself to different levels of analysis and understanding, from laypeople to those who are 'rooted in knowledge' or 'endowed with clairvoyance'. One of the verses that Ibn Rushd repeats most is: "*Reflect, o ye who have been endowed with clairvoyance*" (Q 59:2).

Erroneous Approaches

Now, in the last few decades, at least two major approaches to Science and Islam have appeared on the scene and have seduced Muslims in large numbers: a) *I`jaz `Ilmiy*, the "miraculous scientific content in the Qur'an and the Sunna (Prophetic Tradition)"; b) 'Sacred Science' ('Scientia Sacra'), the neo-traditionalist philosophical approach developed by Seyyed Hossein Nasr and his followers. What do these two approaches say about Islam and Science, and why do I say they are erroneous?

---

[45] The full title of Ibn Rushd's book is: *Fasl al-Maqal fi ma bayna-sh-Shari`a wa-l-hikma mina-l-Ittisal* ("The Definitive Discourse on the Harmony between Religion and Philosophy").

I'jaz `Ilmiy

The popular school of the "scientific miraculousness of the Qur'an and the Sunna" claims that many verses of the Qur'an and hadith of the Prophet (Peace Be Upon Him), if read and interpreted 'scientifically,' express in semi-explicit ways scientific truths that were discovered only recently.

This 'theory' exploded a few decades ago and has quickly expanded to occupy large parts of the cultural landscape of the Islamic world, particularly the Arab part, so much so that a whole industry of 'scientific content' in the Qur'an has sprung forth. A quick Internet search for such literature will bring up books with titles such as *Subatomic World in the Qur'an* (At-Turjumana 1981) and book chapters such as 'Science and Sunnah: The Genetic Code', 'The Grand Unification Theory (GUT): Its Prediction in Al-Qur'an', 'Islam and the Second Law of Thermodynamics' (Syed n.d.), and many more. Articles have been written to show, for instance, that the Qur'an foretold the invention of the telephone, fax, and email (Gulen 1998), radio, telegraph, and television (Al-Jamili 2002) and also some complex (but erroneous) derivation of the speed of light from a few Qur'an verses (Hassab-Elnaby n.d.).

Maurice Bucaille is often incorrectly credited with launching the huge popular interest in this *I`jaz* 'theory', mostly for being French and stating categorically that the Qur'an, unlike the Bible, contains no factually wrong scientific statements; in fact, we often find this *I`jaz* phenomenon referred to in the literature as 'Bucaillism'. In all fairness and accuracy, he was only rarely making the claim of a 'miraculous scientific content' of the Holy Book; for the most part, he was only insisting that it did not contain any scientific errors. And in fact, others many years before him had made the *I`jaz* claim, and with confusion and hype being staples of this whole phenomenon, the fine distinctions and the historical evolution of the trend were often lost.

Today, the *I`jaz* phenomenon has taken alarming proportions by acquiring high-level official support in the form of the 'Commission for Scientific Miracles of Qur'an and Sunnah' that was established in Mecca many years ago under the auspices of the World Muslim League as well as the many international conferences that have been organised on the subject, often under the auspices and personal support of heads of states, prime ministers, and other high officials...

The Commission has organised at least a dozen such international conferences: the 8th in the series was in Kuwait in 2006, the 9th one was in Algeria in 2009, the 10th one was in Istanbul, Turkey[46] in 2011, the 11th one was in Madrid, Spain in 2015, and many regional ones as far away as South America (in Brazil in March 2010, in Egypt in April 2010, Tunisia[47] in 2012, Egypt[48] in 2013, Morocco[49] in 2014, Algeria[50] in 2014 and more to come).[51] Leaders of that World Authority now claim that the evidence of "miraculous scientific content in the Qur'an and the Sunna" that is presented in these conferences is so impressive that many (western) scholars convert during

[46] Organised by the World Agency for Scientific Miracles of the Qur'an and Sunnah, March 11-14, 2011: http://www.eajaz.org/index.php/Authority/The-most-important-achievements. The papers can be found here: https://islamhouse.com/ar/books/342122/

[47] Co-organised by the 'Palace of Science' in Monastir (Tunisia), March 21-24, 2012:. https://wp.me/p9qLgg-7o

[48] a) Conference organised by the University of Beni Soueif (Egypt), March 2-3, 2013: http://www.gomhuriaonline.com/main.asp?v_article_id=73792; b) Conference organised by the University of Mansoura and the World Agency for Scientific Miracles of the Qur'an and Sunnah, April 7-8, 2013: http://el-wasat.com/portal/News-55707076.html.

[49] Co-organised by the College of Science at the University of Tetouan (Morocco), April 25-27, 2014: http://www.presstetouan.com/news8920.html.

[50] Organised by the University of Bordj Bou-Arreridj (Algeria) under the title "Promoting Scientific Research through Qur'anic Inspiration", Nov. 26-27, 2014: http://www.elhayat.net/article10784.html.

[51] An international conference has been announced by the World Agency for Scientific Miracles of the Qur'an and Sunnah and the Qatari Ministry for Religious Affairs for 2014, but no date has been given: http://www.eajaz.org/index.php/component/content/article/11318.

those meetings (Ben Mahfoudh, 2011). There are even conferences on "Miraculous numerical content of the Qur'an"[52] now.

Additionally, the Commission publishes a magazine and releases videos on *I`jaz*, not to mention the countless booklets that have been published by various authors, on such topics as "Qur'anic miracles in geology". Likewise, newspapers and TV channels are full of articles and shows on the subject; indeed, many of the homemade science TV shows tend to be of the *I`jaz* type...

Another recent example of the popularity and official support for this school is the attribution of the Dubai International Holy Qur'an Award (DIHQA) of the "Islamic Personality of 2006" to Zaghloul El-Naggar, one of the stars of this phenomenon, and to Zakir Naik in 2013.

Most alarmingly, curricula at the high school and university levels now routinely contain at least a chapter on *I`jaz*. Indeed, El-Neggar told Stefano Bigliardi in an interview published by the latter in his book, *Islam and the Quest for Modern Science: Conversations with Adnan Oktar, Mehdi Golshani, Mohammed Basil Altaie, Zaghloul El Naggar, Bruno Guiderdoni and Nidhal Guessoum*, that he has convinced "a large number of universities in the Arab world" to offer a course on *I`jaz*, not to mention PhD theses that he examines.[53]

Many scholars have expressed objections to the whole approach, and I presented a thorough critique of the methodology of this school as well as a detailed rebuttal of its most famous claims and examples, including the 'speed of light from the Qur'an' and other stunning claims. The objections can be summarised as follows:

---

[52] The third conference was co-organised by the International Commission for Numerical Miraculousness of the Qur'an and the Center for Qur'anic Studies of Universiti Malaya (Malaysia), Sept. 22-23, 2012: http://vb.tafsir.net/tafsir31444/#. VJ-TOsAA.

[53] Stefano Bigliardi, Islam and the Quest for Modern Science: Conversations with Adnan Oktar, Mehdi Golshani, Mohammed Basil Altaie, Zaghloul El Naggar, Bruno Guiderdoni and Nidhal Guessoum, Istanbul, 2014, p. 128.

(1) Crediting many of the scientific facts that the *I`jaz* proponents tout to the Qur'an when in fact they were known to ancient physicians, philosophers and naturalists.

(2) Often assigning untenable meanings to some of the Qur'anic vocabulary (pulsar is assigned to *al-tariq*; *al-jawar al-kunnas* becomes synonymous to black holes and so on).

(3) Displaying an amazing lack of understanding of essential scientific facts and theories,[54] not to mention of the history of science, which only leads to derision from non-believers.

(4) Promoting a belief that words and verses in the Qur'an carry specific meanings, as opposed to the multiplicity of layers of meanings that Ibn Rushd and others had emphasised.

(5) Giving the Qur'an, or more accurately the exegesists, a veto power over scientific claims or results; this we find in many writings, including on cosmology and biology, as we shall see, when we have by now understood that science must be judged by experimental and observational tests, not by what one verse or another is understood to imply…

To sum up, the *I`jaz* literature is not only replete with incredibly incorrect statements but it is also constructed out of deeply flawed and erratic methodologies. Its extraordinary popularity relates to sociological and historical factors. Indeed, it raises several questions: What kind of understanding does the Muslim world have of science? What level of critical thinking and analysis do we find in the Muslim society (in general) today? Is this due to some eagerness among Muslims today to turn their general defeat in all fields into a position of precedence and superiority and to convince themselves that their holy book, religion, and civilisation are indeed superior?

---

[54] El-Naggar confuses 'dark matter' with 'primordial gas' (the 'smoke' mentioned in the Qur'an) and further thinks that the COBE (Cosmic Background Explorer) satellite detected the 'primordial gas' (El-Naggar, *Min Ayat al-I`jaz al-`Ilmiy, As-Sama fil Qur'an al-Kareem* – 'The Scientifically Miraculous Verses on the Heavens of the Qur'an', Dar al-Ma`rifa, Beirut, 4th ed., 2007, pp. 116-117).

This book is in fact partly an attempt to redress that situation, or at least to prepare a generation of Muslims to think more correctly and confidently about both Science and Islam.

A) *Sacred Science*

"Ever since children began to learn [...] that water is composed of oxygen and hydrogen, in many Islamic countries they came home that evening and stopped saying their prayers. There is no country in the Islamic world which has not been witness in one way or another, to the impact, in fact, of the study of western science upon the ideological system of its youth...."[55]

– Seyyed Hossein Nasr

Sacred Science ('scientia sacra') is the neo-traditionalist philosophical approach that was developed chiefly by the famous Iranian philosopher Seyyed Hossein Nasr (who has lived in the USA for the last 40 years or so). Nasr believes that modern/contemporary Muslim thinkers have accepted modern science too hastily, not having identified its objectionable metaphysical and methodological bases. Chief amongst these being its insistence on naturalism (which is too quickly equated with materialism) and denial of any role—or even the very existence—of the spiritual dimension of man and nature, not to mention God's existence and role in the world. As the quote given above indicates, Nasr believes that the naturalistic descriptions of nature (water is composed of oxygen and hydrogen) has led to an abandonment of worship and spirituality by the Muslim youth and to a general negative impact of western science on the Muslim society.

Nasr then develops a conception of science that is 'sacred', insisting that nature in Islam is itself sacred, as it is (in his claim) imbued with spirits and that one cannot undertake an exclusively naturalistic description of any of it phenomena, since angels and demons

---

[55] Seyyed Hossein Nasr, in a lecture given to MIT students in November 1991; the transcript, with some reproduction errors, is available at http://web.mit.edu/mitmsa/www/NewSite/libstuff/nasr/nasrspeech1.html. See also William Chittick's (supportive) commentary in "Science of the Cosmos, Science of the Soul: The Pertinence of Islamic Cosmology in the Modern World", Oneworld, Oxford (UK), 2007, pp. 99-101.

are intertwined with matter and forces and energy. In this way, everything is united under a new conception of Tawheed (the Islamic unicity principle, usually understood to apply to God only): God, nature, humans or spirits…

This school attracted much interest among Muslim elites first, due to the charisma, eloquence, and novelty of the discourse that its leader, Nasr, developed. Furthermore, many highly educated Muslims, strongly anchored in the Qur'an as a matchless divine text, always hope to see all knowledge under the command and control of the Holy Book and long for a gone-by era when science constituted no challenge to Islam, whether factually or philosophically. The traditionalist school appealed to them emotionally, giving them hope that the Qur'an's supremacy and Islam's dominance as a framework for science and civilisation can be brought back. Today, however, the school has lost its general aura, although it is still supported and promoted by a number of high-level intellectuals.

In my view, the school of sacred science first and foremost rejects science's principle of methodological naturalism, which insists that all proposed descriptions, explanations, and models be solely based on natural causes and effects. By doing so, it is said to be "keeping God out of the picture", looking at the world and nature as if God does not exist. Nasr calls this a "cutting off of God's Hands". But this is a rather simplistic and overly negative view. One can describe this 'methodological naturalism' more positively by seeing God as first sustaining the world through the mere presence of laws in nature, which guarantee order in the cosmos, and secondly acting (indirectly) through the so-called secondary causes, the primary cause being God Himself. Indeed, the rejection of methodological naturalism as a rejection of God is too hasty, to say the least.

But Nasr goes further than that in his critique of modern science and his attempt to redraw it on sacred ground. Indeed, Nasr notes that modern science, being a 'secular' enterprise, is an anomaly with regard to human history. He remarks that the western civilisation is the first one to construct a science, a knowledge and description of nature that negates or at least leaves aside the sacred. He makes a causal link between this fact and the problems that have resulted from science and its applications (technology); indeed, Nasr blames modern science *in toto* for all the ills that can be found in society, from the onslaught on the environment to the debasement of man. He thus calls for the revalorisation of traditional science(s), which he defines as science/knowledge that puts the Divine, the sacred, and man at the centre of all considerations.

Nasr uses the term *scientia sacra* (sacred science/ knowledge) to describe this conception of knowledge. (Nasr insists on using the Latin expression.) He first defines sacred knowledge as that "which lies at the heart of every revelation" and "the centre of that circle which encompasses and defines tradition". In this conception of science, knowledge of nature is holistic and anti-reductionistic and integrates the spiritual realms in its conception of the universe. Ibrahim Kalin, a disciple of Nasr, explains this concept: "Whereas reason by its nature analyses and dissects the world around it into fragments in order to function properly, the intellect synthesises and integrates what has been fragmented by reason."[56] He adds: "Just as the reality of God is not limited to His creation, the reality of the natural world is also not confined to the analysis and classification of natural sciences."[57]

By its very nature, this 'sacred science' differs from modern science in every imaginable way: first and foremost, modern science is very quantitative and avoids dealing with concepts like meaning, purpose, value, beauty, and such, but Nasr insists that these concepts are more valuable, and truer to the nature of various aspects of existence. He readily sacrifices the ideals of objectivity and universalism (of modern science) for the sake of these qualities, which

---

[56] Ibrahim Kalin, "The Sacred versus the Secular: Nasr on Science", op. cit. Kalin comments that: "The distinction between reason and intellect on the one hand, and their unity at a higher level of consciousness on the other, are the two fundamental tenets of the traditional school."

[57] Ibid.

he regards as much more important and relevant to our knowledge and understanding of the world.

In my view, what we have here is a mixing of two domains: the area of rigorous, universal, empirical methodology for the exploration and investigation of nature and the cosmos, and the area of finding meaning in what we discover and learn. The two are primarily different in that the first one is objective while the second is subjective, and they have fundamentally different approaches. Mixing them simply leads to utter confusion. Moreover, whatever one does about meaning, purpose, and adding spiritual considerations, cannot come at the cost of sacrificing large swaths of established science, as Nasr and his followers do by rejecting the Big Bang cosmology and evolutionary biology.

"Say: Travel in the earth and see how He makes the first creation, then Allah creates the latter creation; surely Allah has power over all things."

– Qur'an 29:20

Is Modern Cosmology Acceptable to Islam?

The year 2016 was the 50th anniversary of the death of Georges Lemaitre, the great Belgian cosmologist who introduced the original idea of the Big Bang (later largely developed by various scientists) and who was a Catholic priest. Interestingly, Pope Pius XII seized on the idea to insist that it confirms the Bible's Genesis description of the creation of the world by God, the famous 'fiat lux' ("let there be light"), but Lemaitre warned against making such hasty and improper connections, stressing the need to abide by rigorous scientific methodology, not scriptural interpretations, to confirm or reject a scientific model like the Big Bang.

In the Muslim world, we rarely (if ever) see that kind of methodological rigour, particularly from men of faith, but oftentimes from men/women of science.

We have seen how the *I`jaz* phenomenon has seduced countless Muslims, including too many scientists, who are too happy to make quick and strange connections between various scientific discoveries (from the Big Bang to the genetic code). On the other hand, many Islamic scholars have no hesitation critiquing and rejecting well-established scientific theories, from the Big Bang to the heliocentric solar model, not to mention evolutionary biology.

It may come as a surprise that a number of Islamic scholars reject the Big Bang. (But then again, it may not, since some of them even reject the earth's revolution around the sun…) Why do any *ulamas* reject the Big Bang? Since "it does not fit the Qur'anic description of the creation of the world…" Let's look a bit closer at this issue.

Firstly, there is the 'issue' of which was created first, the heavens or the earth? Sheikh Dr. Marwan Al-Taftanazi (another *I`jaz* specialist)[58] has weighed in on the subject: "The verses 41:9-11[59] decree an established cosmic fact of definite meaning, that the earth after the initial 'separation' was created first, then the heaven was shaped and constructed from the primordial 'smoke'. […] And those among exegetes who, out of a strong urge to conform to scientific theories, tried to put the creation of the heavens before that of Earth, have committed a serious mistake."[60] The sheikh also gives us an explicit timeline for the cosmic creation process: "1) Earth was created in two days after it got separated from the smoky mass; 2) the seven heavens were fashioned in two days; 3) Earth was prepared and

---

[58] Marwan Al-Taftanazi is a relatively young (fortyish) Imam who holds two masters' and one doctoral degrees, who has specialised in I`jazi discourse: produced a 3-volume encyclopaedia and other works, has a regular radio show on the subject and frequently appears on TV in the United Arab Emirates.

[59] "Say: Is it that ye deny Him Who created the earth in two Days? And do ye join equals with Him? He is the Lord of (all) the Worlds. He set on the (earth), mountains standing firm, high above it, and bestowed blessings on the earth, and measured therein all things to give them nourishment in due proportion, in four Days, in accordance with (the needs of) those who seek (Sustenance). Moreover He comprehended in His design the sky, and it had been (as) smoke: He said to it and to the earth: "Come ye together, willingly or unwillingly." They said: "We do come (together), in willing obedience."

[60] Al-Taftanazi, op. cit., p. 171.

made ready to serve humans in two additional days." This scenario he simply takes from an answer given by one of the Prophet's (Peace Be Upon Him) companions, Ibn Abbas, who when asked about the chronology of cosmic events, gave the above timeline series.[61] And if that were not explicit enough, Al-Taftanazi then goes on to give more physical details,[62] declaring that God's Throne was initially above 'water' (from 11:7, which the sheikh takes literally); then God produced "a disturbance in the water, which then foamed and made vapour; the foam remained in the water and was made to coalesce into one earth, which God then split into two earths, while the smoke (vapour) rose and God made the heavens out of it..."[63]

Then there is the 'issue' of the 'primordial smoke', relating to the Qur'anic verse (41:11): "Then turned He to the heaven when it was smoke; He said to it and to the earth: "Come ye together, willingly or unwillingly." They said: "We do come (together), in willing obedience." This has generated tons of writings in attempts to interpret the verse, either to confirm with the Big Bang or to declare an inconsistency between the two.

Sheikh Al-Taftanazi uses some mixed understanding of the Big Bang and describes this 'primordial smoke' from which the heavens were created as an "initial hot cohesive mass"[64] (his wording), which he identifies with Lemaitre's 'primordial atom', even though this expression has not been in use in cosmology for 70 years.

The reason for these misguided objections is the continued attempts to either find scientific information in the Qur'an or to make the Holy Book an arbiter for scientific models and theories. We will also find this to be the reason for a flawed understanding of the world when we review (below) the Islamic views on evolution. As I have explained and will continue to stress, scientific models and

---

[61] Ibid, p. 173-4.

[62] Taken from Muhammad Abu Su`ud's Qur'anic exegesis, "Irshad al-`Aql al-Saleem" ("Guiding the sound mind"), Dar Ihya' al-Turath al-`Arabi, Beirut, no date.

[63] Al-Taftanazi, op. cit., p. 175.

[64] Al-Taftanazi, op. cit., pp. 170-177.

theories will stand or fall on the basis of experimental and observational evidence, not on account of someone's interpretation of Islamic or other scriptures. Data is the only objective and common denominator for all humans to refer to and abide by. Scriptures presents us with a worldview (theistic, spiritual, ethical, humanistic etc.) which gives meaning to this or that discovery and new understanding of the world and the cosmos, but they cannot be substituted for proper, methodical science.

On the subject of the Big Bang, I do not think there should be any quarrel with the scenario that science gives us about the universe's origin and evolution, whether from Islamic or other scholars, simply because there is ample observational evidence and support for the theory (see the side-bar on this in chapter 3). Moreover, if anything, one would imagine religious scholars to hail this theory (as Pope Pius XII did when it first came out) because it certainly seems to support a creation ex-nihilo (out of nothing), which is one of the old arguments for the existence of God, the creator of the world(s).

Nowadays, there are cosmologies being constructed for a 'no-singularity' Big Bang theory (Hawking and Hartle and others), although this would still imply an initial moment of creation. There are also 'pre-Big Bang' models being constructed to try to get rid of that 'initial moment' idea (which is intimately related to the Creator in most people's minds). There is no evidence to support any such 'pre-Big Bang' model, but even if it came to be confirmed somehow, it would still not get rid of the concept of a creator ("who created the matter or energy or laws or universes that gave birth to our universe?"). In fact, I can foresee some Muslims pointing out that the first verse of the Qur'an refers to the 'Lord of the worlds (or universes)', in the plural...

Is Modern Biology (Evolution) Acceptable to Islam?

In November 2011, a story[65] broke in the western media about British Muslim students 'increasingly'[66] refusing to attend biological evolution classes. Even medical students, it was reported, were part of that worrisome development. The story quickly went quasi-viral; even the BBC and Al-Jazeera International ran shows about it. There may have been some socio-cultural factors at play in that specific instance, but the objection to evolution by students is real and can be witnessed in many places.

Indeed, evolution is quite widely rejected by Muslims, including educated people; recent surveys have found about 60% rejecting it outright, with an additional 20% voicing some doubts or accepting it for animals but not for humans. However, it should be noted that it is taught in high schools in countries like Egypt, Iran, Pakistan and other Muslim majority countries. There is some (anecdotal) evidence that many Muslim students and teachers in those places do also reject evolution but pragmatically 'compartmentalise' its study as simply part of the curriculum, without turning it into a socio-political issue. Other (limited) surveys on the views of Muslim physicians in the west (UK and US)[67] and some Muslim-majority countries (Egypt, Indonesia, Malaysia, Pakistan, and Turkey)[68] have shown that large fractions of Muslim doctors reject the theory of evolution, particularly with regard to humans.

Indeed, there is no uniform Islamic position on the theory of evolution. Ever since its earliest formulation by Darwin (and subsequent improvements on it), Muslim scholars have reacted to it with a variety of viewpoints, including sometimes a full acceptance of its

---

[65] http://www.theaustralian.com.au/higher-education/uk-muslim-students-boycott-lectures-on-evolution/story-e6frgcjx-1226208363347

[66] http://www.dailymail.co.uk/news/article-2066795/Muslim-students-walking-lectures-Darwinism-clashes-Koran.html; https://openaccess.leidenuniv.nl/handle/1887/17069

[67] http://wikiislam.net/wiki/Muslim_Statistics_-_Science#Evolution

[68] http://www.scidev.net/global/health/news/complex-islamic-response-to-evolution-emerges-from-study-1.html

scenario on the origin and history of humanity. In such cases, religious scholars insist on a theistic interpretation: God planned that whole evolution, by writing it in the laws of nature, and perhaps even 'guided' it.

But there are also strongly creationist positions in today's Muslim culture, the clearest and strongest one being expressed by Harun Yahya and his group, who for the past decade or more have launched an aggressive campaign targeting Muslims throughout the world, including the UK and France, where lecture tours are organised and books (such as the infamous *Atlas of Creation*) are massively distributed either freely or in subsidised sales. In my previous book, *Islam's Quantum Question*,[69] I presented a detailed critique of the claims made by Harun Yahya.

So if there is a large spectrum of Islamic positions vis-à-vis evolution, why do those students claim that "it is against the teachings of the Qur'an"?

First, that attitude stems from the same methodological confusion I decried above: the Qur'an should not be a reference against which any scientific theory or result is checked; the Qur'an is a book of spiritual, moral, and social guidance; it encourages people to explore the world and fold that knowledge within its theistic worldview. However, it does not claim to present descriptions, much less explanations for how the world works.

Secondly, stating that evolution is "against the teachings of the Qur'an" stems from taking certain stories, particularly the creation story of Adam, literally and accepting the interpretations of the Holy Book by old scholars as the definitive meaning of those verses. As I often tell people, just as we do not reject the sun-centred model of the solar system just because the Qur'an says "the sun rises" and "the sun sets", we must not reject evolution just because the Book says "God created Adam from clay".

---

[69] Nidhal Guessoum, *Islam's Quantum Question: reconciling Muslim tradition and modern science*, London: IB Tauris, 2011, pp. 315-319.

The openness of the Qur'an to (re-)interpretation was recently underlined by Sheikh Yusuf Al-Qaradawi, perhaps the most influential Muslim scholar of the past few decades, who stated that: "If Darwin's theory is proven, we can find Qur'anic verses that will fit with it..."[70] Indeed, a number of scholars have found in the Qur'an possibilities for accommodation of the theory of evolution, both the biological part and the human part. For instance: "And We made every living thing of water" (21:30); "Allah has created every animal out of water. Of them is (a kind) that goes upon its belly and (a kind) that goes upon two legs and (a kind) that goes upon four. Allah creates what He wills. Lo! Allah is Able to do all things"(24:45); "And He created you in stages..." (71:14); "He it is Who created you from clay, then He decreed a term/era..." (6:2).

The idea that the Qur'an can accommodate biological and human evolution has been expressed by a number of Muslim scholars. One must first mention Hussein al-Jisr, an important Lebanese Sunni scholar, who in 1887 published a book[71] in which he carried out a thorough and clear discussion of Darwin's theory from a positive and confident Islamic position. He firmly believed that Islam systematically supports the truth in any area and encourages progressive thinking. According to him, Islam accepts the naturalistic methodology of science, as long as it does not challenge the central principle of a creator. This led him to accept the evolutionary paradigm in principle, citing several Qur'anic verses to show their consistency with it. He even noted that the Qur'an suggests that the creation of life started from inanimate matter.

---

[70] Yusuf Al-Qaradawi, *Al-Shari`ah wal Hayat* (Al-Jazeera TV show), 3 March 2009; transcript and video (in Arabic) here: http://www.aljazeera.net/programs/ religionandlife/2009/2/25/%D8%A8%D8%AF%D8%A7%D9%8A%D8%A9-%D8% A7%D9%84%D8%AE%D9%84%D9%82-%D9%88%D9%86%D8%B8%D8%B1%D 9%8A%D8%A9-%D8%A7%D9%84%D8%AA%D8%B7%D9%88%D8%B1

[71] Hussein Al-Jisr, *Al-Risala al-Hamidiyya fi Haqiqat al-Diana al-Islamiyya wa Haqiqat al-Shari`a al-Muhamadiyya* ("A Hamedian Essay on the Truthfulness of the Islamic Religion and the Truthfulness of the Islamic Canon Law"), Beirut, 1887.

In doing so, Al-Jisr subscribed to Ibn Rushd's twin principles of harmonisation of revelation and reason/science:[72] 1) the "two truths", both coming from God, cannot possibly contradict each other; 2) *Ta'wil* (hermeneutics) of Qur'anic verses must be undertaken whenever the literal reading leads to a disagreement with established truths of nature.

In a recent article,[73] Muzaffar Iqbal (an anti-evolutionist) mentions a number of famous and/or highly respected Muslim scholars from the 1880s to the 1970s who were 'theistic evolutionists' (evolution as a divine plan for creation): Muhammad Abduh, Seyyed Ahmad Khan, Abdullah Yusuf Ali, Fazlur Rahman, Ayatollah Murtaza Mutahhari, Ayatollah Behishti, Javad Bahonar, Maurice Bucaille, Muhammad Hamidullah, Muhammad Iqbal, and others...

By contrast, the late twentieth and early twenty-first-century period in the Muslim world is characterised by the strong fundamentalist, literalist brand of religion that has taken hold. And that is why a large majority of Muslims today, including elites, whether educated in modern universities or religious ones, reject evolution, at least with regard to humans.

The main theological issue for Muslims with respect to evolution is the place of Adam. Indeed, most Islamic scholars to this day understand the creation story of Adam as indicating a special and separate creation of a first full-fledged human being, and many insist that this occurred in a metaphysical 'paradise', not here on Earth. Thus, most scholars find it impossible to conceive of a pre-Adam species or even a possible multiplicity of Adams and lineages, many of which ended up disappearing (e.g. Neanderthals, Java men etc.).

This oppositional stance is due to a literalistic interpretation of the scriptures. In a recent book[74] on the subject, David Solomon

---

[72] See Marwa Elshakry, "Muslim Hermeneutics and Arabic Views of Evolution", *Zygon*, vol. 46, no. 2, June 2011.

[73] Iqbal, Muzaffar, "On the sanctity of species", *Islam & Science*, Vol. 4, No. 2, Winter 2006, p. 89.

[74] Jalajel, David Solomon, *Islam & Biological Evolution – Exploring classical sources and methodologies*, University of the Western Cape, 2009.

Jalajel writes: "The following is apparent from the textual evidence: Adam was created by God directly from earth. Both Adam and his wife were created by God without the agency of parents", and adds: "These are the conclusions that have been reached by all orthodox commentators…" Likewise, Sheikh Bin Baz (the late Grand Mufti of Saudi Arabia) further insisted on the literal truth of the famous hadith that described Adam as being sixty cubits tall.

In opposition to this, the highly respected contemporary Qur'an translator and commentator Muhammad Abdel Haleem underscores[75] the "declared figurative language of the Qur'an" and adds: "In the Qur'anic version, even such details as God forming Adam with His own Hands and the number of days in which He created Heaven and Earth have to be understood, on the instructions of the Qur'an itself, symbolically because elsewhere in the Qur'an we are told that there is *nothing like God'* (42:11; 5:103; and 112:3), and that *'the angels and the Spirit ascend to [God], on a Day that lasts fifty thousand years'* "(70:4).

In another line of argumentation, Shaikh Al-Haddad rejects human evolution on grounds that Adam was a noble prophet. He writes,[76] "Endorsing the presumption that humans evolved necessitates accepting reprehensible beliefs about the noble Prophet Adam, may Allah's peace and blessings be upon him, and that his parents were either apes or ape-like beings! It is to insult the station of prophethood by claiming that Adam was taken care of by human-like baboons. Were Adam's parents able to speak or did they merely grunt?"

Indeed, many Muslim scholars find the spiritual nature of Adam and of humans difficult to reconcile with an evolution from apes, citing Prophet Muhammad's (Peace Be Upon Him) statement that: "Allah created Adam in his own image", which is always understood

---

[75] Abdel-Haleem, Muhammad, *Understanding the Qur'an: Themes and Style*, London: I B Tauris, 1999.

[76] Al-Haddad, Shaikh Haitham, "The Prophet Adam and Human Evolution", n.d., available at: http://www.islam21c.com/theology/2127-the-prophet-adam-and-human-evolution/, retrieved Nov. 18, 2014.

as referring to man's spiritual capacities. That, of course, begs the question of the nature of the soul, which Muslims (following the Qur'an) refrain from attempting to define but consider as a purely human (non-animalistic) characteristic. Thus, many Muslims conclude, at least some aspect of man was created in a special, non-evolutionary manner.

An acceptance of the evolutionary paradigm of humans with other species indeed entails a new conception of Adam and the creation story of humanity. A minority of Muslim scholars have, during the golden age of the Islamic civilisation as well as during modern times, insisted that creation stories in the Qur'an, including that of Adam, be regarded as metaphorical, that the 'paradise' mentioned in that context is a 'garden' on Earth (indeed the Arabic-Qur'anic word 'jenna' simply means 'garden', sometimes an earthly one, in other stories of the Qur'an), that there have been peoples before Adam,[77] the first God-conscious, i.e. spiritual, creature to walk on Earth. Muhammad Shahrour, the original and controversial Syrian thinker, has reconstructed the different episodes in the story of Adam and his children as told in the Qur'an to correspond with different stages of evolution of humanity:[78]

- Hominids standing up (the bipedal posture): Qur'an 82:6-8.

- Development of language: Qur'an 55:3-4.

- Learning of burial: Qur'an 5:31.

- Sacrifice/offering: Qur'an 5:27.

- Spiritual development: Qur'an 5:27.

- Clothing/covering oneself: Qur'an 7:26.

---

[77] Many commentators have insisted that the verse, 'Thy Lord said unto the angels: I am to create a *bashar* (human/humanlike creature) out of clay. And when I fashioned him and breathed into him of My Spirit, then do prostrate before him...' (38: 71--72) clearly implies the existence of 'pre-Adams.'

[78] Shahrour, Muhammad, *Al-Kitab wal Qur'an: qira'a mu`asirah* (The Book and the Koran: a modern reading), Damascus, 1990.

- Finally, Revelation—Man being made God's vice-regent on Earth—and the 'fall' of Adam and Eve from 'paradise'.

Indeed, Shahrour and others (e.g. the late Egyptian Islamic scholar Abdes-Sabour Chahine)[79] have distinguished between the terms *bashar* and *insan* in the Qur'an, both of which are usually understood as 'human being'. For them, the two terms refer to two very different stages of human evolution. Indeed, in the story of Adam in the Qur'an, one finds that each time the word *insan* ('man') is used, there is a clear connotation of "comprehension" (mental capacity), "abstract conception" (of metaphysical entities, in particular) and "intelligence". By contrast, the word *bashar* is used only in the context of the creation of the species, well before it has evolved to *insan* and become mentally capable. In other words, *bashar* is identified with the hominid stage of human evolution or even earlier species of Homo, and *insan* with 'modern man'. Furthermore, the Qur'an mentions the 'breathing of God's Spirit' in the hominid/ homo. Likewise, one must note that one of the key verses above uses the word *ja`il* (making), which is quite different, especially in Arabic, from *khaliq* (creating).

It is becoming clear that the Qur'an does not necessarily stand in opposition to the idea of human evolution. On the contrary, a number of Islamic scholars and thinkers have proposed interesting pathways to reinterpret some verses of the Qur'an in ways that are consistent with both the general message of the Qur'an (man as a flawed, free-willed, and 'special' creature—God's vice-regent on earth) and the scientific facts (the fossil and genetic records) that humans have evolved from lowly origins. The latter idea is also strongly consonant with the Qur'anic verses that remind us that we were created from 'black mud', sometimes described as 'stinking' (to stress the lowly aspects of human origins).

The fact that we have evolved from primates, that at some point we became Homo sapiens, at which point we became spir-

---

[79] Chahine, Abdes-Sabour, *Abi Adam – Qissat al-Khaliqa bayn al-Ustura wa al-Haqiqa* ("My Father Adam – the story of humanity between myth and reality"), Cairo: Dar al-I`tisam, 2nd ed., 2003 (1st ed. 1998).

itual, God-conscious, and capable of interacting with God, turning to Him, praying and seeking guidance, and receiving revelation (teachings, truths), is not a scenario that should conflict with the main Islamic/religious principles. Such as that there is a God, that we humans have a capacity to interact with Him, that there is a purpose for our lives here on Earth, that we have an important role to play (i`mar, literally "to build", which implies civilisation and even participating in God's continuous creation).

We must not cling to old views and conceptions. If, as we Muslims keep claiming, knowledge and science occupy a high place in Islam, then we must embrace it fully and confidently and not turn dogmatic, close-minded, and selective toward theories when they do not conform to old ideas.

We must open our minds to all new ideas. We must be confident that our faith and worldview are robust enough to deal with modernity in its various facets; indeed, new viewpoints can help fine-tune beliefs and worldviews. Islam welcomes all new knowledge and deals with it objectively, even if (as in the case of evolution) it forces us to revise some ancient views.

Does Modern Science Lead Away from God?

> *"Science is not only compatible with spirituality; it is a profound source of spirituality. When we recognise our place in an immensity of light-years and in the passage of ages, when we grasp the intricacy, beauty, and subtlety of life, then that soaring feeling, that sense of elation and humility combined, is surely spiritual.... The notion that science and spirituality are somehow mutually exclusive does a disservice to both."*
>
> *– Carl Sagan*

The last issue I want to address is a general criticism that many Muslims and other believers level at modern science, namely that it is inherently non-theistic. It never refers to God, it attempts to explain everything through natural causes, and in fact a majority of scientists today are non-believers. This fact, we are to be reminded, is very different from how science was understood and practiced during the Islamic civilisation's golden age.

Indeed, the illustrious astronomer Al-Battani had explained that: "By focusing attention, observation, and extensive thought on astronomical phenomena, one is able to prove the unicity of God and able to recognise the extent of the Creator's Might as well as His wide Wisdom and delicate design".[80] Indeed, the Qur'an itself repeatedly draws the attention of humans to the fact that nature and the cosmos do, in their perfection, point toward the Creator and Designer: *"Do they not look at the sky above them, how We have made it and adorned it, and there are no flaws in it?"* (50:6); *"Those who remember Allah standing and sitting and lying on their sides and reflect on the creation of the heavens and the earth: Our Lord! Thou hast not created this in vain! Glory be to Thee"* (3:191); and other verses, sometimes ending with *"Is there a god besides Allah?"*

Modern science, on the other hand, gradually eliminated this tendency to see phenomena in nature as the "work of God". This was *not* done because scientists were atheists—on the contrary, for a long time most scientists were believers—this was done because it was found that invoking God or spirits in various phenomena (lightning, earthquakes, or seizures) tended to stop the quest for explanations of what was really happening. Still, insisting on finding natural causes for all phenomena is not in contradiction with viewing cosmic phenomena as pointing to God's Majesty and Power. Finding natural causes is what science must do, whereas seeing divine power, meaning, and purpose is what religion can provide...

I should note, however, that while specific phenomena are nowadays explained by simple principles and laws of nature, the grander scheme of elegance and fine-tuning of the cosmos for complexity and life (the Anthropic Principle), has shifted the 'signs' that we are

---

[80] Mujahed, M. (2004), "Usus al-Manhaj al-Qur'aniy fi Bahth al-`Ulum al-Tabi`i-yyah" (The Bases of the Qur'anic Methodology in the Study of the Natural Sciences). Jeddah: ad-Dar as-Su`udiyya li n-Nashr wa t-Tawzi`, 2nd edition, p. 100.

called to notice to a deeper, more striking version of the argument from design.[81]

There is indeed a stark contrast between public discussions of the relations between science and religion in the west and in the Muslim world. In the west, a narrative of conflict (between science and religion) continues to prevail: science is rational, open-minded, and progressive; religion is 'magical thinking', rigid, and backward. In the Muslim culture, science is almost an integral part of religion, for it is supposed to lead to God or at least reaffirm the obvious existence and power of God.

In the west, the European Enlightenment produced a general view that science and modernity are synonymous with secularism, if not atheism. Many western scientists and intellectuals today (the biologists Richard Dawkins and Jerry Coyne, the physicists Lawrence Krauss and Sean Carroll, the philosopher Daniel Dennett, the public intellectual Sam Harris and others), have made it their agenda not just to try to push religion out of the public space but to depict it as the biggest hindrance to human progress. They often point to the resistance of many religious people to modern scientific knowledge (Darwin's evolution, in particular) or new vistas (stem-cell research, genetic engineering etc.).

Still, one frequently encounters western scientists who are fervent believers (in one religion or another), who feel no conflict between their religious beliefs and their scientific mindsets. Likewise, one often meets devout Muslim scientists who oppose none of the established and aforementioned contemporary scientific knowledge.

In the west, surveys of scientists' religiosity have been conducted by several groups of researchers, going back to a landmark study in the US by Leuba in 1916. Recent surveys have also been conducted in the US and in the UK among scientists of various levels, including members of the US National Academy of Sciences, the American

---

[81] See my aforementioned book, *Islam's Quantum Question: reconciling Muslim tradition and modern science…*

Association for the Advancement of Science, and the UK Royal Society. Members of such high elites have been found to be much less religious than other academics.

Furthermore, US scientists have been found to be much less religious than the general population: where some 90% of lay Americans are reported to believe in God or some higher power,[82] 40% of American scientists believe in God, 45% do not, and 15% are agnostics; in fact, among members of the high societies, 15% or less believe in a personal God or a higher power; a notable exception is physicians: 3 out of 4 are reportedly believers (see the survey published by Ecklund and Scheitle in 2007).

Until now, however, we have only had surveys from the US and the UK. Those must then be interpreted with the western historical and social contexts in mind, i.e. with the aforementioned science-religion conflict narrative that has prevailed in the western discourse.

But now, for the first time, a large-scale, international study is (as I write) being conducted about the attitudes of scientists toward religion around the world. Professor Elaine Howard Ecklund of Rice University (USA) and her collaborators have launched a survey of 20,000 scientists in France, Hong Kong, India, Italy, Taiwan, Turkey, the UK and the US.

I was recently invited to a seminar where results from the surveys in the UK and India were presented, after roughly 2,000 scientists were surveyed and some 100 were interviewed in depth in each country. Contrary to the UK, where non-belief is prevalent among both scientists and the general public (but more so among the scientists), only 11% of Indian scientists said they do not believe in God or a higher power, compared to 2% of the general public, and only 19% of Indian scientists never attend any religious services.

---

[82] Elaine Howard Ecklund & Christopher P. Scheitle, Religion among Academic Scientists: Distinctions, Disciplines, and Demographics, *Social Problems*, Vol. 54, Issue 2, pp. 289–307, 2007.

So while we eagerly await the results of the study from other countries, particularly Turkey for at least one Muslim context, it is already clear that the attitudes of scientists toward religion vary highly from one social and cultural environment to another.

The studies also show that the conflict narrative between science and religion that the western popular culture has been deluged with is not dominant on the ground; indeed, only 38% of UK scientists describe religion as being in conflict with science. In fact, many scientists openly hail the positive influence that religion often has on the practice of science, particularly in terms of ethics; few see religion as 'interfering'. Indeed, there are several areas where the two can cooperate: environmental issues and the fight to eradicate poverty, to name just two.

But for such cooperation to take place, everyone must adopt an attitude of humility. As the Qur'an reminds us, "You have been given but little of knowledge..." This is a core Islamic belief: God is not only infinite wisdom and knowledge; He is the source of knowledge and wisdom.

Science does not lead to atheism, that is only a propaganda line that is promoted by the new atheists (Dawkins and his group), who are a very small minority and who try hard to promote their ideology. Indeed, this is a purely ideological stance; there is nothing in science that implies atheism. As I have explained, science is objective and neutral; it only describes nature and the cosmos; it is completely left to us to give meaning to the discoveries and new knowledge that science gives us, and such meaning can easily—in fact we Muslims and believers say 'can better'—be constructed when harmony between religion and science is sought.

CHAPTER 6
·················
Islam and Science in Our Future World

وَالسَّمَاء رَفَعَهَا وَوَضَعَ الْمِيزَانَ

أَلاَّ تَطْغَوْا فِي الْمِيزَانِ

وَأَقِيمُوا الْوَزْنَ بِالْقِسْطِ وَلا تُخْسِرُوا الْمِيزَانَ

وَالأَرْضَ وَضَعَهَا لِلْأَنَامِ

سورة الرحمن، الآيات 10-7

"He raised the heaven and established the balance
That you would not transgress the balance.
Give just weight – do not skimp in the balance.
And the earth He laid out for all living creatures."

Qur'an 55: 7-10

Momentous Developments

SCIENCE IS MAKING PROGRESS AT an accelerated pace. Extraordinary advances have been made over the last 10 or 15 years and more and greater ones are on the way that will raise our knowledge of the world a few more levels and transform the way we live, think and worship. I have mentioned a few recent astonishing developments in science, such as the discovery of more than 3,000 exoplanets in the last 10 years or so. It is worth remembering that just 20 years ago we didn't know of any planets outside our solar system. Now we are zooming in on planets that resemble Earth in its physical features and cosmic environment (habitable zone around a 'good' star), such that the chances for life to appear/or make an appearance there are reasonable. We are also preparing instruments and techniques that will detect the signatures of life on faraway planets if they exist. I come back to this topic below and consider its implications. I further delve into this topic below and consider its ramifications for religious beliefs.

Another very recent development was the detection of gravitational waves for the first time since they were predicted 100 years ago by Einstein's General Relativity theory. This breakthrough opens a new window to the universe by extending our observational capabilities beyond electromagnetic waves, just like radio telescopes and balloons and satellites extended our view of the universe beyond the visible light spectrum. However, I don't see any important philosophical or theological implications to this cosmic revolution beyond the wonder and awe in front of this extraordinary universe that God has created.

The 20th century is always described as the century of physics, with its revolutionary theories (relativity, quantum mechanics, big bang, to mention only these), but the 21st century is widely expected to be the century of biology, not because the science is about to witness any radical developments, but because bio-technology is beginning to introduce world-changing techniques, such as genetic engineering, with small or big modifications to various organisms (with gene-altering tools such as CRISPR-9 having become available to any small bio-lab in the world). Furthermore, the imminent usage of stem cells for medical applications, and most of all the impending explosion on the scene of 'synthetic biology', sometimes called 'artificial life' for stronger emphasis, which is the creation of genes and DNA from scratch with subsequent insertion into the nuclei of cells, making them do whatever we programme them to. The ethical and religious implications of these techniques are obviously quite huge, and conferences are already being organised to come up with guidelines on how to govern their usage.

As if that were not enough, we also have to contend with the impending arrival of (strong) artificial intelligence looming on our world. We already have 'smart' computers and machines that can predict what we want just from our first few keystrokes, machines that can learn from our habits and adjust their responses accordingly, but we will soon have machines that will be able to 'think' on their own and take decisions without our consent. What limits we set to their abilities will be interesting to see: more capability will make them more useful to us but more independent, with all the risks attached to that; less ability will prevent us from taking full advantage of their potentials.

And when bio-technology and artificial intelligence are merged, sometime this century, then we will have created biological robots, or androids, with a host of ethical issues emerging. We are already beginning to contend with ethical issues pertaining to animals; for that we need to decide what really distinguishes humans from animals, and what minimal or maximal rights animals should have compared to us. Soon we will have the same questions raised for artificial biological bodies resembling humans, having as much if not more intelligence as humans, and perhaps having learned and developed emotions and morals...

I cannot address all these issues here; I only want to point to them rising over the horizon. In this chapter, I want to limit myself to topics that are already a part of our world at present.

The Search for Other Earths

"Are we alone?" and "Is there life elsewhere?" are questions that have been described as the most important ones facing science today. Indeed, until very recently, these questions remained in the realm of speculation; today we have the tools to address them methodically, step by step.

In the last few years, scientists have been more and more frequently announcing the discovery of 'other earths', or at least planets that are about the same size as Earth and orbit a star in a region where the temperature could be moderate (i.e. a few tens of degrees Celsius), thus allowing water to exist in liquid form, a key condition for the existence of life (as the scientific consensus goes). Indeed, liquid water, though it is not the only such substance, is by far the best medium for molecules to assemble into more and more complex compounds, leading (in principle) to the formation of DNA and RNA molecules, the holders of information and instructions for all life that we know of.

Several of those planets are nearby, between 10 and 100 light-years away from us—next door by astronomical standards—thus allowing for future detailed telescopic studies of their atmospheres (assuming they have one) and even their landscapes (if they really resemble Earth). That will give us additional clues and evidence of any life and activity there with the gases that relate to life (e.g. oxygen, ozone, or methane) in abnormal concentrations.

Indeed, for life to exist somewhere, the planet (or possibly a good moon of a planet) must not only be in the right zone around its star, it must have the right size (for it to have an atmosphere). Both the star and the planet must be stable (if the star erupts too often with radiation, it will kill off any budding life on the nearby planet), and hopefully have mild and regular seasons on the planet (from a nicely inclined axis, like Earth's). We are not yet able to determine which exoplanets have such favourable characteristics.

We are at a critical juncture of the search for life elsewhere. If the nearest thousand stars, with all their planets, are conclusively found to harbour no life at all, then the odds of life existing in our galaxy will be extremely low, if not nil. But if we do find even primitive life in one of our neighbouring star-planet systems, then the Milky Way (with at least 100 billion stars) must statistically be full of life, some of it probably quite advanced elsewhere. Either way, it will be an extraordinary conclusion for science to reach and an interesting (though in my view not overly vexing) theological question to ponder. The more fascinating issue, for science, religion, and human culture, is whether there are highly intelligent creatures out there...

What about Aliens, Anybody There?

Many people, from having watched so many science-fiction and alien movies, are convinced that there are intelligent and advanced extra-terrestrial species out there. When pressed for an argument, they often reply that it doesn't make sense to have zillions of galaxies, stars, and planets, all devoid of intelligent life. As a character in the (great) movie *Contact* put it: "If it is just us, seems like an awful waste of space."

I am often asked whether I believe in the existence of extra-terrestrials. My immediate reply is: "It is not a question of belief; it is a scientific question, just like 'are there black holes?' and 'are there other earths?', and it must be addressed by rigorous scientific research." Of course, I realise that the question also has a philosophical, existential, and even theological aspect: did God create this whole universe for only one species (us), or are there many others, some of whom perhaps much more intelligent and advanced than us? What would that imply?

The first attempt to address the question scientifically was about fifty years ago when Frank Drake, an American astronomer and pioneer in the field, assembled a group of scientists to try to come out with a programme to address the question. And just to kick-start the discussion, he listed the factors that determine the probability of existence of intelligent extra-terrestrials: the number of planets around other stars; the fraction of those that could support life and produce intelligent, technologically advanced civilisations; and how long these could survive and be detectable by us. Multiplying those factors gave what is now known as the Drake Equation, which has become one of the most famous equations ever.

But as anyone reading this short list of factors can quickly realise, it is difficult to quantify them precisely, and so the result was (and still is): the number of such extra-terrestrial civilisations is somewhere between 'only one' (humanity) and millions. The only way to find out was thus to search.

And thus was born SETI, the Search for Extra-Terrestrial Intelligence programme, which scans the sky for any radio or laser signals containing a message. Fifty years of searching has yielded nothing. The cosmos is huge; signals could be coming from very far (and our equipment is limited); and it is difficult to analyse all the radio emissions that we detect from the galaxy, let alone the rest of the universe.

Bring in crowd-sourcing—even before the word was coined! In 1999, the public was called upon to participate in the SETI@Home programme by downloading software that makes a person's computer analyse SETI data (from the host, the Space Sciences Laboratory at the University of California, Berkeley) any time the computer is idle. More than five million people have participated from all over the world (233 countries), logging over two million years of computer time. Still no ETs...

There is a whole line of debate about this 'eerie silence' (as Paul Davies elegantly summed it up)[83]. The great physicist Enrico Fermi had, from the start, asserted that aliens do not exist, at least not in our galaxy: "Where are they?" He asked. By that, he meant that if aliens exist in our galaxy, they will have had millions or billions of years to develop higher intelligence and technologies (since life appeared on Earth about 8 or 9 billion years after the formation of the Milky Way, other stars and planets would have appeared well before, and life would have evolved on one of them long before here), they would thus have already found us (with their advanced technologies), and their presence or passage would have left some traces. This became known as the Fermi Paradox, and many books and articles have been written about it, supporting or rebutting it.

Counter-arguments to the Fermi Paradox include that perhaps those highly intelligent species have not noticed us (since we've only recently emerged and become somewhat advanced), or that perhaps they are just not interested in visiting us.

But if they don't come to us or contact us, perhaps we should try to contact them or at least make ourselves heard. The most appropriate method for reaching out to aliens, an approach known as Active SETI, is to send out radio signals and laser beams with information about us. The famous physicist Stephen Hawking warned

---

[83] Davies, Paul (2010), *The Eerie Silence*, Boston, New York: Houghton Mifflin Harcourt.

against doing this, for our civilisation would then be in danger of invasion by far superior alien species.

Contrary to what sci-fi movies tend to imply, we must always keep in mind that aliens, if they exist anywhere, may not resemble us, in form, technology, philosophy (intentions) etc. But if they do exist and are highly intelligent, they are probably technologically, but also mentally and morally way superior to us. Paul Davies believes aliens are extremely likely to be 'post-biological' creatures, by which he means 'reengineered', with largely enhanced capabilities, particularly brain power, up to any fundamental limits imposed by physics. Long before that, ETs will have 'transitioned' to super-machines with what Davies calls 'godlike mega-brains'. "Why would such an entity bother to contact us?" he asks. In his view, such aliens would not even have any interest in the physical universe, let alone us. They may perhaps spend their time solving elaborate math problems, proving new theorems, entirely living a life of the mind...

What theological/religious implications would such an existence have? In Davies's view, "any theology with an insistence on human uniqueness would be doomed." This, in principle, also applies to Islam, at least in the views of Islamic scholars who have not imagined us possibly being like primitive creatures compared to those 'mega brains', although many Muslims not only accept the possibility or probability of the existence of ETs but even claim that the Qur'an alludes to them (Qur'an 26:29). But Davies remarks: "Although slow to change, religion is very adaptable." He compares this new challenge to that posed by Darwin's Evolution, which also questioned Man's special status within most religions; he concludes: "The discovery of advanced extraterrestrial beings would represent a far more explicit threat of the same nature, and prove that much harder to assimilate."

What remains then is to assess the probability of such an encounter. That's anyone's guess. No doubt, this is a fascinating subject.

Back on Earth...

"Corruption has appeared on land and sea
Because of what people's own hands have wrought,
That they may taste something of what they have done;
And that hopefully they will turn back."

Qur'an 30: 41

Down here on Earth, two important issues have come to the fore of human concerns that relate to science and perhaps somewhat to religion. Our biggest problems are of course wars, refugees, epidemics (HIV, Ebola, Zika etc.), poverty, malnutrition (including lack of drinkable water), lack of proper housing and electricity in many places, unavailable education for millions of children worldwide, and other such huge issues that are still in need of our pressing attention. And science can surely help address some if not all of these; at least problems like epidemics, malnutrition, and the dearth of electricity can be addressed by science (e.g. by solar or wind power), assuming the financial resources are made available, and perhaps issues like education for all can be helped by science using technological solutions (cheap computers, educational CDs etc.)

But the two inter-related problems that have come to dominate the debates in recent years are climate change ('global warming') and the need to find new energy solutions, as we near the end of the oil era. These are issues where science plays an important but perhaps not central role, since they first and foremost fall in the domain of political and economic policies. Still, we have seen social and even religious leaders step into the debates, for the simple reason that humanity's future is at stake, with potentially disastrous effects, such as droughts, deluges, floods, mosquito proliferation, large population displacements etc.

Let us look briefly at those two topics: climate change and energy sources.

"Our scientific power has outrun our spiritual power.
We have guided missiles and misguided men. "
– Martin Luther King, Jr.

Climate Change - Global Warming

Every year now, the weather 'goes crazy' in various ways and in different parts of the world. We have all seen stunning pictures of frozen lakes and snow-covered monuments in places that used to rarely get much snow, and temperatures have gone off the normal ranges in many places, with surprising deep freezes in some cases.

In cases like the latter, people often ask why such cold waves are happening when we are supposedly undergoing a 'global warming'. First, the phenomenon is called *global* warming, and indeed, while one region or another might get a surprising deep freeze, other regions are now regularly experiencing heat waves. In fact, when maps are released for global temperatures each month, records are being broken more and more frequently. It is estimated that since the 19th century (when temperatures started being recorded systematically), our planet's average temperature has risen by about 1 degree, which is huge. In some places e.g. the northern American states of Wisconsin, Minnesota, North and South Dakota, and Vermont, temperatures have undergone an increase of almost three degrees. In 2014, Siberia's winter was warmer than usual by 8 degrees. And in the Arabian Peninsula, snow storms have occurred a number of times in normally arid desert regions.

The moral of the story is twofold: a) there is an overall increase in global temperatures (global warming); b) the climate changes differently in various parts of the world, with some experiencing cold or heat waves, and some regions receiving huge amounts of precipitation (rain, snow), which can be disastrous.

Scientists have worked hard to try to extricate the phenomenon of global warming, with its natural and artificial (human-induced) causes as well as its varied and dangerous consequences. But it seems that they have not done nearly as well at explaining it to the public.

Every few years, the UN-appointed Intergovernmental Panel on Climate Change (IPCC, which received the 2007 Nobel Peace Prize with Al Gore for work done to raise awareness about the problem), releases a new report on climate change. It gives the latest measurements (temperatures, sea levels etc.) as well as the best, most sophisticated computer simulations of the global climate, trying to predict temperatures and precipitations in various regions in the decades to come.

It is important to stress that there is a near-consensus on two facts: a) that the planet is steadily warming; b) that this is due to human-produced greenhouse gases (mainly carbon dioxide and methane, although water vapour contributes quite a bit when the heat evaporates water from seas and oceans). It is the latter point (that the warming is caused by humans) that is disputed by a small minority of 'sceptics', including some scientists, although they tend to get a disproportionate amount of media coverage.

The IPCC, which was established in 1988 by the World Meteorological Organisation and the United Nations Environment Programme, is comprised of several working groups, with expert contributors participating from over 130 countries, with more than 800 contributing authors and over 2500 scientific reviewers. It has so far produced five 'assessment reports' (1990, supplemented in 1992, 1995, 2001, 2007 and 2014), which are based on solid scientific papers.

The IPCC reports' conclusions have become stronger and stronger, describing the warming of the planet as 'unequivocal' and declaring it as 'very likely' (more than 90% probability) due to human actions. Moreover, it predicts that should our carbon dioxide emissions remain unchanged, by the end of this century sea levels will have risen by 15 to 60 cm, with an additional 10 to 25 cm if the recent polar ice sheet melting continues.

This general scientific conclusion has been adopted by dozens of national and international organisations, including the American Association for the Advancement of Science, the US National Research Council, the European Science Foundation, the European Academy of Sciences and Arts, the International Council of Academies of Engineering and Technological Sciences, and at least 32 national science academies which have issued declarations (sometimes jointly) confirming the global warming trend and its human origins.

The latest IPCC reports also present a number of reasonable solutions for everyone to start implementing, solutions which revolve around two main ideas: a) reducing carbon dioxide emissions by adopting cleaner energy sources; and b) modifying our lifestyles (housing, transportation etc.) to reduce energy consumption. The IPCC recommends adopting natural gas and shunning oil and coal, in addition to renewable energies such as solar and wind power. Nuclear energy, however, remains a divisive issue among scientists and environmental activists.

Islamic Perspectives

In August 2015, forty or so Islamic scholars, social activists, and policymakers gathered in Istanbul to discuss climate change and other environmental and planet-related issues. They produced a historic, bold, well-informed, well-thought, and wide-ranging declaration[84] that set clear targets on greenhouse emissions (phase out by 2050) and energy sources (complete replacement by renewable sources by 2050).

The Declaration reminded Muslims and the rest of humanity of their religious duties and responsibilities to safeguard the planet that we have been entrusted with, "What will future generations say of us, who leave them a degraded planet as our legacy? How will we face our Lord and Creator?" It also pointed to a host of en-

---

[84] http://islamicclimatedeclaration.org/islamic-declaration-on-global-climate-change/

vironmental, ecological, and socio-economic issues that require our immediate and serious attention (Global climate change; contamination and befoulment of the atmosphere, land, inland water systems, and seas; soil erosion, deforestation and desertification; damage to human health, including a host of modern-day diseases etc.), and presented a list of Islamic moral and behavioural principles to live by for the betterment of our planet and human society.

Commenting on the Declaration, Hakima el-Haite, Morocco's minister for the environment, underscored the religious basis for the call and programme that the leaders issued: "It is an emotive call for a spiritual fight against climate change that will be very important for Muslims... I think that the right way to make this sort of call is through the Qur'an."[85]

The importance of the Islamic perspective was further stressed by the United Nations' climate chief, Christina Figueres: "Islam's teachings, which emphasise the duty of humans as stewards of the Earth and the teacher's role as an appointed guide, illuminate pathways to take the right action on climate change."[86] Therefore, it is clear that one of the duties of the learned Muslim is to be aware of our impact on this world that we were gifted and entrusted with to take care and to preserve to the best of our abilities; this in fact is a duty for Muslims.

---

[85] https://www.theguardian.com/environment/2015/aug/18/islamic-leaders-issue-bold-call-rapid-phase-out-fossil-fuels
[86] Ibid.

Islamic Principles for Humanity and Planet Earth
(Islamic Declaration on Global Climate Change)

- God created the earth in perfect equilibrium *(mīzān)*: By His immense mercy we have been given fertile land, fresh air, clean water and all the good things on Earth that makes our lives here viable and delightful; the earth functions in natural seasonal rhythms and cycles: a climate in which living beings—including humans—thrive.

- Humans have caused corruption *(fasād)* on the planet due to a relentless pursuit of economic growth and consumption, resulting in: a global climate change, which is our present concern, in addition to: pollution of the atmosphere, land, water, and seas; damage to human health, including a host of modern-day diseases.

- Although we are but a miniscule part of the divine order, we are exceptionally powerful beings, and have the responsibility to establish good and avert evil in every way we can.

- Intelligence and conscience behove us, as our faith commands, to treat all things with care and awe *(taqwa)* of their Creator, compassion *(rahmah)* and utmost good *(ihsan)*.

- Prophet Muhammad (Peace Be Upon Him) set a wonderful example on how to behave with respect to other creatures and to the environment:

  o Prohibited the killing of living beings for sport, taught people to conserve water even in washing for prayer, forbade the felling of trees in the desert and the mindless destruction of animal habitat.

  o Established inviolable zones *(harams)* around Makkah and Al-Madinah, within which native plants would not be felled or cut and wild animals would not be hunted or disturbed.

  o Established protected areas *(himas)* for the conservation and sustainable use of rangelands, plant cover and wildlife.

- o Lived a frugal life, free of excess, waste, and ostentation.

- o Renewed and recycled his meagre possessions by repairing or giving them away.

- o Ate simple, healthy food, which only occasionally included meat.

- o Took delight in the created world.

- o Was, in the words of the Qur'an, "a mercy to all beings."

- Adopt a set of ambitious policies to restore the environment order, including:

  - o Phasing out greenhouse gas emissions as early as possible and no later than the middle of the century.

  - o Recognising the moral obligation to reduce consumption so that the poor may benefit from what is left of the earth's non-renewable resources.

  - o Committing to 100% renewable energy and/or a zero emissions' strategy as early as possible, in order to mitigate the environmental impact of activities.

  - o Investing in the creation of a green economy.

Energy Issues: Shale Gas etc.

If fossil fuels are ruining our climate and environment, it seems logical and simple to insist on turning to cleaner energy sources, preferably renewable ones (solar, wind, hydro- and geo-thermal, etc.). Nuclear energy, as I have mentioned, remains a divisive issue, particularly after the Fukushima near-disaster (and 20 years ago, the devastating Chernobyl nuclear reactor meltdown).

Solar energy is perhaps the best alternative so far, even though the efficiency of solar cells remains low, which forces solar panels to be huge in order to deliver reasonable amounts of energy, particularly in areas of the globe where the sun shines infrequently. Wind energy is likewise limited to regions that experience strong winds regularly enough. And geo- and hydro-thermal energy is only available to the rather few locations on earth where volcanic and underground activity supplies large amounts of heat that can be extracted.

And so the world recently turned to shale gas and oil, for two reasons: a) first and most importantly because it is available in huge quantities in many countries and its extraction is/was cheap enough to produce large profits; b) shale gas, although a fossil fuel, produces much less carbon dioxide than oil. In the last 5-10 years, it has changed the global energy balance and prospects. In particular, it has allowed the United States to essentially become energy independent and even a producer. It has created hundreds of thousands of jobs in the USA, and possibly millions worldwide. And it has allowed new fossil fuel producers, such as Argentina, to enter the market.

Shale gas is extracted by 'fracking', the hydraulic fracturing of rocks deep underground to make them release their fossil fuel contents. But this technique has been shown to have significant 'secondary effects' both on the environment and on people, and thus been banned in the UK, France and Germany. By contrast, in the US, 30,000 shale gas wells were drilled between 2011 and

2014. In Algeria, where some studies estimated the reserves as second only to the USA's, the government launched an ambitious programme to use this technique to raise its total gas production by 40 percent, but large protests erupted in the region where the wells were drilled and continued for months.

Indeed, fracking has been found to produce numerous mini-earthquakes. But there are other, more serious threats that opponents of fracking raise and sometimes document in shocking detail.

Most importantly, shale gas wells come with a definite risk of leakage of the water and chemicals that are used in the fracking process. The leaked fluids can then contaminate the underground water supplies, with very dangerous health consequences on humans and animals; many videos have documented those effects. Another serious problem is that fracking uses very large amounts of water to crack the rocks by high-pressure injections. That water is taken from natural reserves underground, which are often vital resources in regions where water is scarce and difficult to pump up. Moreover, the water is filled with chemicals and nuclear products to help the high-pressure fracturing of the rocks, and the elimination of the wastewater carries risks of leaks, spills, or sometimes just easy, illegal dumping in nearby lakes.

Observers tend to agree that if done right, fracking can represent an economic boon for many countries. 'Done right' means making sure that the gas is fully captured and that the by-products of the process are totally recovered and dumped deep underground, without any risk of leakage or spilling. This requires both high technology and strict monitoring of the companies that undertake this.

Life and Humans in the Universe

"There is no animal on the earth, or any bird that wings its flight, but is a community like you."

Qur'an 6: 38

One of the most important discoveries of modern science (or at least modern physics and cosmology) is the fine-tuned and special disposition of our universe to complex life, intelligence, and consciousness. John Wheeler, the illustrious physicist, put it best: "A life-giving factor lies at the centre of the whole machinery and design of the world."[87]

Indeed, over the past half century, scientists have discovered that many features of our Universe are astoundingly fine-tuned to our existence, or to the emergence and evolution of life more generally. Indeed, if the parameters and laws that make up the physical cosmos had been drawn at random, the probability that they would have values allowing for life and intelligence to appear (at some point in time and space) would be ridiculously small, one in billions of billions of billions...

Many thinkers have recognised this discovery as an extremely important one; it is often referred to as the Anthropic Principle— the universe's predisposition for life and the human species. Countless articles and books have been written about this in recent times; a very clear and complete account of the topic was presented by Paul Davies, the well-known scientist-philosopher,[88] in *"The Goldilocks Enigma: Why is the universe just right for life?"*[89]

Now, the idea that the world is well designed and made adequate for humans is both old and ubiquitous among many cultures, including the Islamic one. This 'design argument' did suffer serious

---

[87] John Wheeler, Foreword to John D. Barrow and Frank J. Tipler's *"The Anthropic Cosmological Principle"* Oxford University Press, 1986, p. vii.

[88] Paul Davies has published, among many other books, *"The Cosmic Blueprint"*, *"Are We Alone?"*, and *"The Mind of God"*; in 1995 he was awarded the Templeton Prize for Progress Toward Research or Discoveries about Spiritual Realities.

[89] Paul Davies, *"The Goldilocks Enigma: Why is the universe just right for life?"*, London: Penguin, 2006.

blows in the wake of the Copernican and Darwinian revolutions, but contrary to the elites, laymen overwhelmingly continued to believe that humans are special and that Earth and perhaps the universe were designed (directly or indirectly) as cradles for humanity.

And indeed, the discovery of the fine-tuning of the universe, brought back 'man' to the centre, so to speak. As Wheeler commented on that extraordinary and historic shift in view:[90] "Man? Pure biochemistry! Mind? Memory modelable by electronic circuitry! Meaning? Why ask after that puzzling and intangible commodity? [...] What is man that the universe should be mindful of him?"[91] But a few lines further, Wheeler retorts: "No! The philosopher of old was right! Meaning is important, is even central. *It is not only that man is adapted to the universe. The universe is adapted to man.*" (Emphasis added.)

Indeed, it was no longer a matter of seeing beauty and harmony in nature, nor even a set of smart observations such as the temperature, pressure, gravity, and environment of Earth being 'just right'[92] for our existence and activity; it was now a question of the very foundations of the universe. The parameters and physical laws upon which everything was built, all of which were found, time and time again, case after case, to be finely tuned to the existence of life in general, and higher intelligence and consciousness as well.

This fits perfectly well with the Islamic worldview in general. Indeed, in addition to the argument from design that we find ubiquitous in the Islamic culture (that Allah has designed everything perfectly well and for good purpose), the idea of harmony between

---

[90] Wheeler, op. cit.

[91] Ibid.

[92] Barrow and Tipler (op. cit., p. 143) make a special reference to the two seminal books by Lawrence J. Henderson (Harvard professor of biological chemistry), *"The Fitness of the Environment"* (1913) and *"The Order of Nature"* (1917); indeed, Henderson had noted the very special regulation of acidity and alkalinity in living organisms; CO_2 dissolved in water is the regulator of neutrality, and water is absolutely unique as a regulator and conductor of heat (having a very large specific heat capacity and conductivity), in its surface tension, in dissolving other substances, and in many other properties.

humans and nature can also be found, as Ibn Rushd for instance notes that: 1) all that exists is in harmony with humans; and 2) this can only be the result of an Agent who wanted it so. He gives examples of heavenly and earthly objects, with their most-appropriate characteristics.[93]

Now, Muslims may insist that since humans were created to worship God, nature is then simply here to facilitate this function (physically, emotionally, and spiritually) by helping us to reflect upon it and perhaps come to know God through it. Muslims may then read these fine-tuned universe and anthropic principle developments and be tempted to see them as confirmation that we are 'evidently' at the centre of the universe, and perhaps the universe was indeed created for us. But one must always remember that the universe is much larger than our limited view and perspective, and the purpose of creation as a whole is a divine reason largely outside our understanding.

Biotechnologies and Islam

The reason for the above (brief) review of the recent discovery of the fine-tuning of the universe and its extraordinary predisposition to life is to help formulate an Islamic paradigm, or at least an Islamic perspective, on bioethics with its current and future potent developments.

Indeed, if we find difficulties in discussing stem-cell research and its applications or genetically modified foods and organisms, how are we to handle much more challenging topics such as 'gene drives'[94] (systematically removing a 'bad' gene from an entire spe-

---

[93] Ibn Rushd in "Al-Kashf `an Manahij al-Adillah fi `aqa'id ahl al-milla" ("Uncovering the Demonstrative Methods in Islamic Doctrine", translated into English as "Faith & Reason in Islam"), cited by Marc Geoffroy, op. cit., pp. 139-140.

[94] See Jennifer Kahn's TED talk (Feb. 2016): "Gene editing can now change an entire species – forever": https://www.ted.com/talks/jennifer_kahn_gene_editing_can_now_change_an_entire_species_forever

cies), 'synthetic life'[95] (sometimes referred to as 'artificial life'), animal 'de-extinction'[96] projects (bringing back dinosaurs and other animals, and perhaps in the future dead humans), technologically modified or 'augmented' or 'enhanced' humans[97] (sometimes referred to as 'transhumanism'), and even 'immortality'?[98] The definition and the sanctity of life are being seriously impacted, with implications on 'beginning of life' and 'end of life' issues, such as conception, abortion, and euthanasia.

I believe that Muslims must take full consideration of the integrated paradigm of the cosmos that has emerged from modern science: our existence cannot be dissociated from that of the rest of life on Earth and its history, and this cannot be viewed separately from the natural elements that surround us and relate to us. After all, we are made of the same elements as Earth, and our DNA is based on the same biochemistry as that of the rest of life on Earth, including plants and animals. In fact, we now know that many other animals have intelligence (sometimes quite advanced), some of them have language (not nearly as sophisticated as ours, of course), some can make tools and build things, some have family structures and express sadness when one of theirs dies, etc. In the eternal words of the Qur'an, "There is no animal on the earth, or any

---

[95] For discussions of 'synthetic life' and ethics, see for instance: Cho & Relman, "Synthetic 'Life,' Ethics, National Security, and Public Discourse" *Science* 329:38-39, 2010; "Unveiling 'synthetic life'", Craig Venter's TED talk http://www.ted.com/talks/craig_venter_unveils_synthetic_life.html (2010); Ethical Issues in Synthetic Biology, a project of the Hastings Center: http://www.thehastingscenter.org/Research/Archive.aspx?id=1548.

[96] See, for instance, the Lazarus Project, which is conducted at the University of Newcastle, Australia, and which was named as one of the Top 25 inventions of 2013 by TIME Magazine.

[97] See, for instance, the 'Augmented Human International Conferences Series' since 2010: http://www.augmented-human.com/; Report from the workshop on 'Human Enhancement and the Future of Work' of the Royal Society, the Academy of Medical Sciences, British Academy, and Royal Academy of Engineering (March 2012):http://royalsociety.org/policy/projects/human-enhancement/workshop-report/.

[98] See the project on 'The Science, Philosophy, and Theology of Immortality' at the University of California, Riverside: http://www.sptimmortalityproject.com/.

bird that wings its flight, but is a community like you" (Qur'an 6: 38). Clearly this must affect our view of animals, at the very least, and life more generally.

This also should give a new, grander understanding of the "Preservation of Life" principle of *Maqāsid al-Sharī`ah*. The principles of the theory of *Maqāsid* are well known: a) the whole Sharī`ah aims at benefiting mankind (in this world and the next); b) behind all laws are rational principles that can be inducted; c) the laws are not objectives in themselves, they can be transcended in cases where their strict application leads to problems while the objectives can be better fulfilled in other ways.

I believe that the principles of *Maqāsid* (including but not limited to "the preservation of life, mental faculties, lineage, etc."), coupled with a renewed and enlarged worldview that is based on a thorough understanding of the universe as revealed by modern science, can help us Muslims formulate a holistic and proactive ethics system that can be applied to or meshed with the emerging and challenging fields of biological and informational technologies.

Genetically Modified Organisms (GMOs)

People are often confused and worried about GMOs. On the one hand, they hear about possible risks from such organisms (who knows what unintended effects the genetic modification may have) and they don't trust agro-industrial companies; on the other hand, they hear that this can help protect crops from pests and wild herbs, multiply yields, and help reduce famine and diseases.

First, it is worth stressing that there is no credible scientific evidence about negative GMO effects on animals, humans, or the environment. All major scientific organisations (the American Medical Association, the US National Academy of Sciences, the British Royal Society and many others) have issued statements stressing that GMOs-based crops pose no greater risk than 'naturally' grown crops in terms of their effect on the human body.

Secondly, there are indeed important benefits to using GMOs: the protection against insects, droughts, and extreme temperatures, as well as the growth of plants (like 'golden rice') that have artificially been fortified with some vitamins that combat specific diseases. Indeed, 'golden rice', through the production of beta-carotene, remedies Vitamin A deficiency, which blinds 500,000 children worldwide annually.

Thirdly, GMO-based crops are both cheaper (for the farmer and the consumer) and more bountiful than their natural counterparts.

Opponents of GMOs, however, invoke the Precautionary Principle (a sophisticated formulation of "better safe than sorry", "an ounce of prevention is worth a pound of cure", and "first do no harm") and demand strong proofs that there are indeed no negative effects. They point to some studies that have indicated such effects (e.g. the appearance of 'superweeds')—although those studies have been rebutted—and insist that it is too early to guarantee the absence of any dreadful long-term effects of GMOs-based products.

Additionally, some ethical and even religious arguments have been invoked, such as the unlawfulness of 'playing God', as in the case of the green-fluorescent cat that was genetically produced 'for medical tests'.

While the fraction of citizens who express strong concerns about GMOs (even in Europe) has been decreasing lately, and scientists overwhelmingly endorse the usage of these organisms, this debate is not about to disappear. This is one important topic where scientists, religious scholars, policymakers, public advocacy groups, and the media must all play a constructive role to improve the general understanding of the issue, prevent any panics and lead a healthy discussion around it.

Genetic Engineering and Synthetic Life

Discussions of genetic engineering, cloning, stem-cell research and their applications have become commonplace. A basic familiarity and understanding of these terms and the issues they raise is essential for a proper discussion to ensue. This is especially true for educated people, religious leaders, and policymakers in particular.

Clearly, genetic engineering raises a host of ethical and religious questions:

1. Should we allow ourselves to 'edit' animals? In which cases? (We already 'edit' plants genetically.) How do we define 'bad genes'? Which diseases should be dealt with genetically instead of the classical methods? How do we ensure that no (major) unintended consequences occur in such cases?

2. Should we allow ourselves to 'edit' human cells? (The technology already exists, and some forms of it are already practised by some labs, at least in selecting the 'best' chromosomes of embryos…) Where do we draw the line between 'fixing' our flaws and 'enhancing' our bodies (including our brains)?

3. Should cloning be allowed? For humans as for animals? Is it so beneficial as to outweigh its moral drawbacks? What are the moral concerns?

The field of Islamic Bioethics has quickly matured in recent times, with numerous papers, books, conferences, projects, and encyclopaedias. Muslim scholars have looked back into the principles of Shari'ah to guide them in presenting answers to the above questions.

The major principles that Muslim scholars set in this regard include the following:

❖ Clear Qur'anic injunctions must be upheld.

❖ Agreed-upon teachings of Prophet Muhammad (PBUH) must be followed.

❖ Consensus of scholars (to the extent that it occurs) should be upheld.

❖ Well-known juridical rules, such as the following, should be applied:[99]

> ➢ the principle of precautionary preventive approach (*sadd al-dhara'i`*), i.e. forbidding or discouraging acts that are likely to lead to harmful consequences.

> ➢ human needs are divided into essential, necessary, and complementary: they are assigned relative priority (including budgetary priority) in this order.

> ➢ avoiding harm takes priority over bringing good, and the lesser of two harms must be chosen if both harms cannot be avoided.

> ➢ necessities overrule prohibitions, that is when in urgent needs (say famine), prohibitions (for example of eating pork) are suspended.

> ➢ public interest overrules private interest.

Applying these principles, H. Hathout reaches the following conclusions:[100]

❖ Genetic engineering is rejected on the basis of the Qur'anic reference (4:119) to Satan foretelling God that he will tempt humans into tampering with His creation. But "an exception is made when used to produce medicines or other material to alleviate suffering and illness."

❖ Cloning is rejected because it "is a reversion to the most primitive form of asexual reproduction." Additionally, the process requires a high rate of foetal wastage before a clone is born. Furthermore, if cloning becomes widespread, family and social relations will very likely be strongly disturbed...

❖ Stem cell research can be allowed because it uses very young embryos, and these (according to Hathout and many other Muslim scholars) "do not possess the same

---

[99] H. Hathout, "An Islamic perspective on human genetic and reproductive technologies", Eastern Mediterranean Health Journal, Vol. 12 (Supplement 2), 2006, S22 – S28.

[100] Ibid.

rights as a foetus", especially when their usage is for the purpose of saving or healing human lives.

The above are the views expressed by Hathout in his paper. They do not necessarily constitute a consensus and definitive Islamic position on these issues, and there are a number of views on them, but the above do represent typical views. There is no doubt that these fast-evolving topics require more *Ijtihad* (scholarly efforts to come up with novel solutions that fit the general spirit of Islam) from Muslim scholars in manners that benefit from the expertise of biologists, ethicists, jurists, and others.

In his recent paper 'Islamic Bioethics in the twenty-first century',[101] Muhammed Ghaly, who specialises in the subject, reviews the field and attempts to highlight avenues that require more attention and effort. The following are his main critiques and recommendations:

> ➤ Agreeing with Henk ten Have (2013), he writes: "The greatest part of the contemporary Islamic discourse on bioethical issues has been focusing on the so-called "'detailed rulings (*ahkam tafsiliyya*)' in order to see if a specific medical practice (e.g., abortion, cloning, stem-cell research) is permissible or prohibited from an Islamic perspective. This 'narrow' approach, which focuses on the branches of Islamic jurisprudence (*furu' al-fiqh*), can be effectively widened once the higher objectives of Sharia (*maqasid al-Shari'a*) are also accommodated and integrated in the field of Islamic bioethics."

> ➤ Agreeing with Willem Drees (2013), he writes: "most of the bioethical discussions in the Islamic tradition focus on how people relate to normative verses from the Qur'an, Sunna and Islamic jurisprudence" instead of some more general, philosophical 'natural law' ethics...

> ➤ "A better integration of Islamic bioethics into the broad 'religion and science' discourse" is needed. For this, Islamic Bioethics "should be broadened by involving specialists in

---

[101] M. Ghaly, Islamic Bioethics in the twenty-first century, *Zygon*, vol. 48, no. 3 (Sept. 2013), pp. 592-599.

(Islamic) theology and philosophy of religion besides the experts in Islamic law."

> Finally, agreeing again with ten Have, Ghaly advises Islamic Bioethics to try to integrate into a 'global bioethics', by searching for global ethical principles which focus on the values that are shared by all human beings.

There is no doubt that biological issues in general, and biotechnological topics in particular, are raising moral, ethical, and religious issues that human culture in general, and Islam and other religions in particular, need to contend with, particularly as these fields evolve so quickly and new applications and implications appear more and more frequently. This is a challenge for scholars, policymakers, and all educated people for the years to come...

CHAPTER 7

General Conclusion:
What to Take from All This

*"I am among those who think that science has great beauty.
A scientist in his laboratory is not only a technician: he is also a
child placed before natural phenomena which impress him like
a fairy tale."*

– Marie Curie

What Science Brings to Humans

I STARTED THIS BOOK BY mentioning the high status that Islam accords to science, or knowledge more generally, under the rich and multi-dimensional concept of `ilm. And in the second chapter, as I reviewed the evolution of science from ancient to medieval to modern, I devoted a few pages to the thousand years of scientific activity that took place during the Islamic civilisation, from the eastern lands (Baghdad, Bukhara, Khwarezm, Rey, Jaipur) to the western regions of Andalusia and the Maghreb. I mentioned briefly some of the main reasons that made science/knowledge flourish so magnificently during that long period and throughout that wide region.

Why does Islam encourage science so strongly? I think the reasons can be presented under three headings:

1) ***Knowing God through His creation.*** The Qur'an is very strong on this point; let me mention just a few verses (several commentators, e.g. Muhammad Abdus Salam, the first Muslim

Nobel Prize winner in the sciences,[102] have noted that roughly one eighth of the Qur'an refers to nature and the cosmos, encouraging people to contemplate, to explore, to reflect and to comprehend):

❖ *"And among His Signs is the creation of the heavens and the earth, and the variations in your languages and your colours: verily in that are signs for people of knowledge."* (30:22)

❖ *"Say: Contemplate what is in the heavens and the earth."* (10:101)

❖ *"Say: Travel in the land and see how He originated creation."* (29:20)

❖ *"He who created everything and ordered it in exact measure."* (25:2)

Al-Biruni (973–1048), one of the greatest scientists of that entire era, spoke clearly of his faith, but did not let it influence his science. He explicitly stated that the motive behind his research in the scientific fields is Allah's verses: *"Those who reflect on the creation of the heavens and the earth (and say): Our Lord! Thou hast not created this in vain! Glory be to Thee…"*(3:191)

Similarly the illustrious astronomer Al-Battani (850–929) had written: "By focusing attention, observation, and extensive thought on astronomical phenomena, one is able to prove the unicity of God and to recognise the Creator's might, wisdom and delicate design."

2) **Elevation of humans through knowledge and rigorous thinking** (getting rid of superstitions, requiring proof etc.)… In this regard, we can cite hadiths (or ahadith) and statements from the tradition:

❖ "An hour's contemplation (or study) of nature is better than a year's adoration (of God)."

---

[102] Abdus Salam shared the Nobel Prize in Physics with Steven Weinberg and Stephen Glashow in 1979 for successfully unifying the electromagnetic interaction with the weak nuclear force into one theory.

❖ "The ink of the scholar is more sacred than the blood of the martyr."

The rigorous thinking was stressed by some of the earliest Muslim thinkers, for instance:

❖ Al-Kindi famously said: "Our goal must be to garner the truth from wherever it may come, for nothing is of higher priority to the seeker of truth than truth..."

❖ And Avicenna, on the importance of requiring proof: "He who gets used to believing without proof has slipped out of his natural humanness..."

3) ***The need for science in people's lives.*** I mentioned in the brief review of science's history (Chapter 2) that one of the main factors that pushed Muslims to develop at least some branches of science (astronomy, algebra, geometry, arithmetic, and trigonometry, medicine, architecture etc.) was to help people live their lives and even perform their religious duties more easily. I mentioned how Al-Khwarizmi (ca. 780 – ca. 850), when he introduced the new mathematics of algebra, explicitly and immediately gave its applications in daily life, from commercial to inheritance and *zakat* (religious alms) calculations. Likewise, the need to determine prayer times in the direction of Qibla/Mecca from different, faraway places, as well as the construction of crescent-based calendars, led to the development of spherical trigonometry and astronomical knowledge. And last but not least, medicine was an obviously beneficial field, also helped by a hadith from the Prophet (PBUH) stating: "God put [out there] a cure for every disease he created", in other words, "go and find it."

All three of these general reasons strongly show why science is so important in Islam and what it brings to humans—from spiritual to everyday benefits.

But what we have also learned, particularly in Chapter 3, is that Modern Science brings a strong emphasis on rigorous methodology, trying to ensure that we do not just produce 'theories' that suit our preconceptions or inclinations and that all results can be tested and confirmed by different people and in different environments—in other words that scientific claims must be fully objective.

The main ideas that I have tried to communicate to the reader about modern science can be summarized as follows:

1. Science successfully explains natural phenomena through rigorous investigation and proper and extensive testing.

2. The critical arbiter of any scientific claim is not expert authority or common sense but experimental evidence, strong theoretical underpinning, and consistency with other established knowledge.

3. Scientific *theories* are not propositions/hypotheses; they are large frameworks containing empirical knowledge (facts), laws (established to the extent possible), and connections with the rest of the field.

4. Theories can be modified and improved as new empirical knowledge becomes available; every once in a while (rather rarely), a theory is replaced by a greater, more sophisticated one that is able to encompass the old one (explain all the previous data and include the laws known until then), but also explain the new information that could not be addressed by the old theory. These cases are known as 'scientific revolution'.

Having said this, and I cannot stress enough the importance of comprehending these important methodological aspects of modern science, I want to also acknowledge that there are human elements in science. After all, science is performed by humans, who all carry their own mental flaws and are explicitly or implicitly affected in their thinking and their work by their backgrounds and experiences. Let me review this briefly.

The Human Elements in Science

Science is a human endeavour. It is performed by humans, with their personal and collective aspirations and flaws. Scientists must neither be idolised nor mistrusted as freaks who are both power-hungry and deviant in their goals. Fraud has occurred many times and continues to occur, but considering the millions of scientists worldwide (past and present), fraud, especially the deliberate and wilful type, tends to be very rare exceptions. Scientists do sometimes, either consciously or unconsciously, discard data that does not suit their preferred models or theories, sometimes they may even 'correct' some experimental measurements (which they'll attribute to 'instrumental error') so as to fit their expectations.

However, and very importantly, one must always recall that science is a collective endeavour; all good science is peer-reviewed and must be repeatable. No result is accepted, adopted, and built upon by the scientific community if it has not been checked and reproduced by others, preferably in different settings and conditions. This is known as the 'repeatability' criterion or principle of the scientific endeavour. Therefore, any errors, whether conscious or unconscious, are corrected in due course, that is **the power of the collective scientific process**. Hence, the idea that somehow the scientific community deliberately uphold a wrongful 'theory' for ideological reasons is pure nonsense. Evolution or any other theory could never be promoted by so many scientists in so many universities and countries if it wasn't a strong, highly convincing set of evidence explained by a robust theoretical framework and making predictions that continue to be confirmed upon testing. I want to make sure that the reader becomes very clear on this aspect of today's science.

Another aspect of science that is often weakly realised is the humility that scientists must carry and display at all times. Both in their research and in their pronouncements (to their students and to the public at large), they must always keep in mind that we humans know so little and are prone to error. A humble "*I don't know the answer to this,"* uttered by a scientist actually raises his/her stature and leads to greater respect and trust. The public will be more inclined to believe scientists' pronouncements on other occasions when, from time to time, they are heard to say: "I don't know". This aspect of science needs to be stressed and practised much more widely by everyone in all parts of the world.

Further to the issue of humility, we must also keep in mind that science makes progress over long periods of time and in a non-linear manner. By this I mean that scientists sometimes take a wrong route; they collectively adopt a theory based on the best information available at the time, but new data may come to strongly disturb that 'collective wisdom' and force them to take a new route. Referring back to the diagram in Chapter 2 of how science progresses over time toward Truth on various topics, we see that in some periods (usually short, but not always), science actually moves in a direction away from truth.

And last but not least, it is important to realise that science has become more and more inter- and multi-disciplinary, sometimes even combining natural and social sciences. Many examples can be cited in this regard: environment problems, education and psychology, human development, biomedicine, ecosystems, etc. These research fields address how we live, learn, and work. But such multi-disciplinary and holistic topics remind us that on many fronts today we can only make progress collectively; few of us have enough expertise or resources to conduct almost any research which is why 95% of papers published today have several authors.[103]

How Not to be Mistaken: the 'Baloney Detection Kit'

Rigour and correctness are not easy to guarantee, even for scientists. I've mentioned in Chapter 3 some of the common errors that laypeople and even students make when dealing with scientific

---

[103] The average number of authors on the most cited papers in recent years was about 4.

information, for example, mistaking correlations for causations and exaggerating the statistical significance of a survey result or of an experimental measurement. Moreover, there are a number of reasoning errors that so many people, including well-educated ones, routinely make, such as: the confirmation bias; the clustering illusion; the availability bias; the overestimation of one's knowledge; the low but non-zero probability of certain events; the false-dichotomy approach; the cognitive dissonance effect; the difference between median and mean; the small-numbers' effect; the cherry picking approach etc.

There are entire books that address these reasoning errors; a recent and hugely popular one is Rolf Dobelli's *The Art of Thinking Clearly*.[104] So here I will simply give a short list of mental checks that we all need to remember to apply whenever we come across some 'scientific' information, to make sure we are not fooled (or fooling ourselves) or simply mistaken. (Carl Sagan called this approach and a similar list he produced: "the baloney detection kit".)[105] Try to always ask yourself the following 7 questions:

1. What is the evidence supporting the claim? Search for critiques of the claim and weight the arguments of the opposing party. Do not accept claims just because they fit your preconceptions or worldview.

2. How objective and reliable is the source? Is there any indication of an agenda in the claim or its source? Do not fall into the common 'argument from authority' mistake ("this is an 'important' person, hence we must accept his statements").

3. Has there been any *independent* confirmation of the claim? This is an integral part of the modern scientific process, (peer reviewing and independent confirmations).

---

[104] Rolf Dobelli, *The Art of Thinking Clearly*, London: Sceptre, 2013.
[105] Carl Sagan, *The Demon-Haunted World: Science as a Candle in the Dark*, New York: *Ballantine Books*, 1997.

4. Are the effects being described as correlations rather than causal effects? As we have seen, "correlation is not causation".

5. Is the result being reported statistically significant? As I explained in Chapter 3, all scientific results come with some measurement uncertainty/error, and new, different results may or may not be significant depending on the differences and the sizes of the uncertainties.

6. Can the claim (hypothesis) be 'falsified' i.e. tested in order to prove it (or at least provide strong support for it) or reject it (find its predictions to be false)? As I previously explained, for a hypothesis to be scientific, it must be 'falsifiable' i.e. 'testable'. Always ask for the predictions of the hypothesis and wait until others (preferably experts not affiliated with it) have had a chance to replicate the results, observationally, experimentally, or even theoretically (analytically or numerically).

7. Is there a simpler explanation for the effect or the result? As per 'Occam's Razor', simpler explanations tend to be more correct than more complicated ones, though this is not always the case.

Essential Scientific Knowledge

In Chapter 4, I presented "all the (basic) science that you need to (or should) know", a brief review of the essential scientific knowledge in Physics, Astronomy and Cosmology and Biology. The reason I limited myself to these (big) domains of science and did not extend the review to other fields, e.g. geology, neuroscience, etc. was twofold: a) the above topics have witnessed huge revolutions in modern times and produced full-fledged theories (Big Bang, Evolution) that have often represented challenges to religious views; b) while the neurosciences are currently producing a revolution in how we understand the brain and the mind, I have left that topic aside due to my total lack of expertise in it, and am also awaiting for the dust to clear and new paradigms and their implications to emerge.

What were the main results of this essential science review? Here I summarise them in a few bullet points:

1. The physical universe is built on atoms (made of particles), and interactions between them involve radiation (electromagnetic and other fields). Understanding atoms and radiation has allowed us to explore and understand vast areas of nature, such as the Earth and the Sun, accurately describe their processes (past and present), determine their ages and trace their histories since their formation, as well as predict their futures.

2. Progress in Astronomy and Physics has allowed us to understand the solar system, ascertain how the earth and other planets revolve around the sun, understand the sun and the stars, discover the billions of galaxies that make up the observable universe, with vast distances and a bewildering zoo of cosmic objects. We have also discovered how the universe is finely tuned in its building blocks, parameters, and laws for life to exist and evolve. Had gravity, light or nuclei had slightly different characteristics, no life, humans or even complex inert objects would have existed at all.

3. The universe was born, created in a singularity (a point where all matter, energy, space and time were concentrated) some 13.8 billion years ago. The Big Bang theory is able to describe the evolution of the universe from that initial point/moment forward; it makes predictions that have been checked and found to be correct.

4. Life appeared on Earth some 4 billion years ago. We have yet to discover life of any kind, even bacteria, anywhere else. (We defined life as any organism that is able to sustain itself energetically and to reproduce.) On Earth, life has evolved over long periods of time, with complex creatures evolving

from simpler predecessors, producing the entire beautifully diverse spectrum of life forms (plants and animals) that we see on our planet. Human beings are part of this grand creation process, occupying a top niche in an immense tree of living organisms, all sharing a common biological structure (cells, DNA, genes) and biomolecular processes applying to all living organisms.

But I also insist that despite the recent exponential growth of our knowledge of nature, the cosmos, and of the human (and other) species, what remains to be known is infinite compared to the (astounding) knowledge we have gathered, particularly in the 20th century. Important developments await Physics, Astronomy and Cosmology and Biology (not to mention other fields) in the 21st century, on the conceptual and theoretical front (formulation of a coherent quantum gravity theory, understanding how life emerged from inert matter, etc.) as well as on the observational and experimental fronts (discoveries of earth twins, life elsewhere in the cosmos, mastery of nuclear fusion energy, mastering various aspects of genetics etc.).

The future of science promises to be even more amazing than its recent past…

> *"The existence of a limit to science is, however, made clear by its inability to answer childlike elementary questions having to do with first and last things – questions such as 'How did everything begin?' 'What are we all here for?' 'What is the point of living?'"*
>
> *- Sir Peter Medawar*

Why Should Science Care About Religion?

As a Muslim Scientist, I spend much time and expend much energy trying to convince Muslims and other believers to take Modern Science seriously, with all its methodology and results—and its limits.

The reverse exercise, to try to convince scientists and other educated people that religion should be taken seriously, is more difficult, for several reasons. Firstly, because science can often claim whole swaths of *established knowledge*. Today, no one can doubt that matter is made of atoms and particles, that life evolved and produced a vast tree of species, or that the universe has expanded from a singularity and is today made up of hundreds of billions of galaxies, each made up of hundreds of billions of stars, most of which have planets around them, etc.

On the other hand, religion, while having developed branches of knowledge, with methodologies and references, cannot claim to present realms of *established knowledge*. Still, religion can present an ensemble of highly respectable and beneficial ideas that even hardline scientists can appreciate and find useful for humanity, if not for themselves.

But what do we mean by 'religion'? We need to distinguish between 'faith', 'spirituality', and 'religion'. 'Faith' is the belief in something or several things (a creator, a divine force, a spirit, life after death, revelation etc.) without being able to prove that in any objective way. 'Spirituality' is a feeling that there is some activity within us that is not purely material or at least happens at a higher plane than our simple bio-psychological phenomena. 'Religion' is an organised system of beliefs (theology), practices (rules and rituals), and relations, at both individual and community levels.

Most religions, western and eastern, including Islam of course, have developed rather advanced and sophisticated theologies. And most of them have seen an 'evolution' in their theological and jurisprudential (*Fiqh*, in Islam) systems, on account of the evolution and progress of human society, thought, and knowledge. I believe that theology and the rest of religion must be enriched with what modern science brings e.g. our new view of the cosmos.

Now, assuming that this effort has been made on the part of Religion, why should Science take the latter seriously? What is there to gain in doing so? Wouldn't science and humanism be sufficient for the progress of humanity?

Recently, more and more, science and its practitioners have sought to expand the space of investigation and explanation to include all human life and society. This is generally labelled as 'scientism' (often considered a rather pejorative term). This tendency is partly due to the propensity of human societies, despite modern critiques, to place scientists on a pedestal, thereby implying that they possess deeper understandings of the whole world and thus should be entrusted with all our issues to address.

But even scientists with this kind of imperialistic tendency know that our view of the world (nature, human life, society) cannot be limited to the scientific perspective. Indeed, art has always existed and no one has sought to get rid of it simply because a rainbow can easily be explained by physics or music can be recorded as 0s and 1s. Likewise, philosophy is not about to disappear even as some of its topics of old have been taken over by science. Similarly, religion addresses a dimension of human life and thought that can rarely be illuminated by science.

When we ask believers what religion brings to them, we usually hear the following: a personal purpose and meaning to one's life, a perspective on things, a sense of identity, an emphasis on love as the most important factor in life, a communal bonding and support, moral guidance and compass, and a greater ability to cope with death and disasters.

When we ask scientists what science brings to them, we often hear ideas such as 'a unified worldview,' whereby the universe 'makes more sense.' Indeed, the cosmos inspires feelings of awe, wonder, and mystery that are often described as 'spiritual' even by atheists. But what believers find in religion is a harmonious explanation for all of existence, with its physical and metaphysical dimensions, mental, spiritual, relational and communal. It also unifies the ideas of life and death.

The universe is mysterious and perplexing. Of course, we must not fill our inability to comprehend some aspects of it by postulating ad hoc beliefs. Still, it is reasonable to construct a worldview that can give meaning to the phenomena that one observes (unimaginable vastness, layers upon layers of complexity, staggeringly intricate effects stemming from a handful of simple laws or principles) in harmony with the rest of human life and history.

Many religious academics and scientists have also indicated that their beliefs help them deal with the question of what it means to be human. Again, due to the large spectrum of beliefs that people hold, 'what it means to be human' can range from 'being in the image of God' to 'having a spirit' or even just 'a higher level of consciousness.' In any case, one can see that such personal beliefs, whether constructed for oneself or taken from the teachings of one's religion, can be helpful in this matter.

Furthermore, a number of religious scientists have stressed that their beliefs provide them with stronger ethical principles both in their lives and in their scientific practice. The question of ethics in science is a vast issue that has been discussed at length by various thinkers and organisations, but what higher principle must be set in order to derive ethical regulations and standards has never been obvious. And so here, as in the question of humanness, believers state that (their) religion constitutes a frame of reference and a set of guiding principles to help them derive rules of practice.

To sum up, science, at least in the parts that one must regard as established, must be accepted and upheld by all, believers and non-believers, particularly educated people. Believers must strive to make faith, spirituality, and religion, as sophisticated, open and up-to-date (with the latest knowledge) as possible. Then (and only then) can science and religion have much to bring to one another in cohesion and to humanity.

My final words to you, dear reader, are that we cannot ignore science, with its methods and results; it brings so much to humanity, as I explained at the beginning of this final chapter. But religion too can provide very positive contributions to humanity, provided that it gets rid of some of its followers' irrational and unacceptable beliefs and practices.

There is so much for the world to gain in having science and religion in harmony...

"Science without religion is lame, religion without science is blind."

– Albert Einstein